Seaside Front Line

Seaside Front Line

A DIARY OF EVENTS AND INCIDENTS

AT

FRINTON, WALTON, KIRBY & GREAT HOLLAND

1939–45

Geoff Rayner

FORAY

Mendlesham, Suffolk

Also by the same author
One Hurricane – One Raid, Airlife Ltd.

First Published 1996

FORAY
Vine House
Front Street
Mendlesham
Suffolk

ISBN 0 9528186 0 4

Typeset by Type Align Graphics
Printed by The Lavenham Press Ltd.

Front cover illustration:
A beach scene at Frinton, September 1940 I.W.M. H3986

INTRODUCTION

The area covered by this diary is fortunate in not being renowned for any particular military event in history, but as the dark clouds of war gathered in 1939, followed swiftly by the possibility of invasion, its strategic significance in the defence of the East Coast, came to the fore just as it had when Napoleon had threatened and, to a lesser extent, during the First World War.

Between the Rivers Thames and Colne, the vast tracts of Essex coastal salt marshes form a natural defence against invasion from the sea. The Tendring coast provides the first suitable landing place north of the River Thames and is a potential back door to securing the port of Harwich – a valuable asset for any invading force, being one of very few deep water ports on the English southern North Sea coast.

The prominence of the Naze cliffs, extending out into the northern Thames Estuary, ensured their use for siting of one of the Air Ministry's early radar stations: part of the chain that was to play such a vital part in the aerial conflict of Battle of Britain. Later in the air war that same prominence became many a pilots' first glimpse of friendly territory when nursing a damaged aircraft back across the southern North Sea.

A wide variety of the various phases of the war were experienced in the local area. Early on there was the toll from magnetic mines at sea; sending small craft to the beaches of Dunkirk; the creation of a coastal defence zone; preparations to defend the coastline against invasion and the Battle of Britain taking place overhead.

Later there was the construction of secret decoy sites; the establishment of a 'battle school'; training of anti–aircraft gunners and attacks by 'tip and run' raiders. Towards the end there came the rain of V1 'doodle–bugs' and V2 rockets and the impact of anti–aircraft batteries despatched to the coast to counter them.

All the time there was the continuous military presence along the shore and the constant bombing from aircraft jettisoning their loads before making off across the sea: in total there were over a thousand air raid alerts. Then there was the involvement of the lifeboat, and organisations such as the Home Guard, A.R.P., Naval Patrol Service and Coastguards.

At the cessation of hostilities in 1945, it was in the District's interest to remove the legacy of military occupation and return the coast to normal as quickly as possible. Together with post war development, which has more than doubled the population, it has ensured that today there is little physical evidence of what took place all those years ago; the most durable features being the few remaining concrete pillboxes and some memorials. Beyond that the events of those times remain only as memories for the local people who were there at the time.

Prior to the Second World War, much of the accommodation in Frinton and Walton was as seaside second homes or as holiday accommodation. The permanent residential population was therefore a small proportion of what exists today. Evacuation of children and the creation of a 'coastal defence zone' which encouraged non essential civilians to leave the area, meant that the population was reduced even further. The younger men and women also departed for the forces and so it was a much reduced local population that experienced the war years in the local area. After the passage of fifty years there are few today who can recall the events first hand and hence one of the motives for creating this volume.

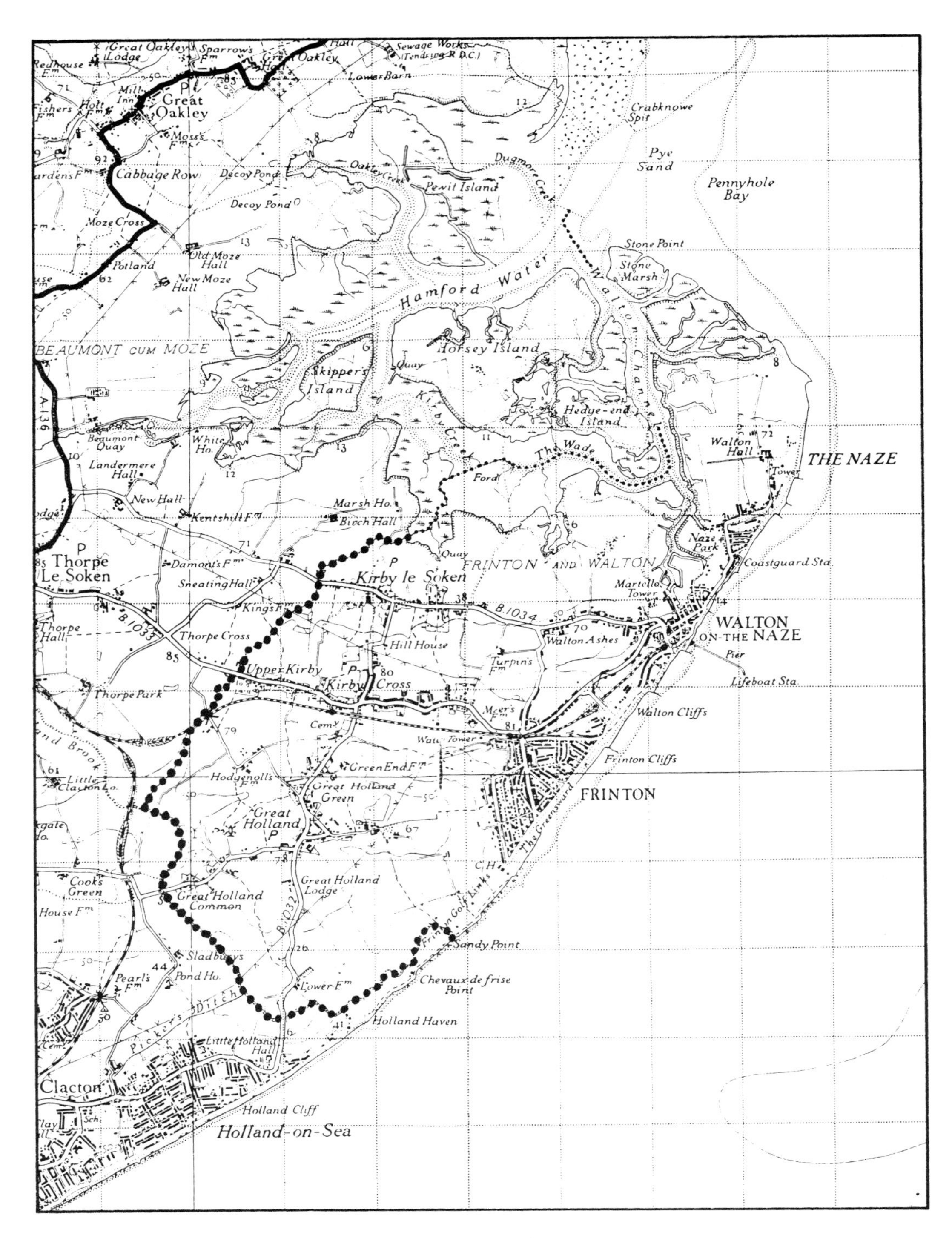

Frinton & Walton Urban District

Based on a 1940s Ordnance Survey Map

The objectives are to inform those who were not in the area, what went on locally, during one of the most significant periods of the 20th century and also to provide a solid framework against which memories of particular events may be placed. After the passage of fifty years, the memory can confuse and merge time and place. It is hoped that the production of this 'diary' will stimulate those who can elaborate on the events recorded, to add their own recollection of events and so enrich the local history record. The author will gladly act as a reference point for such recollections so that a collection of such material may be deposited in the archives of the Frinton & Walton Heritage Trust. Alternatively the Trust may be contacted direct through the Maritime Museum at Walton or the Railway Gate House at Frinton.

Incidents and events described are those which took place within, above and offshore of the former Frinton & Walton Urban District, which between 1934 and 1974 was the civil administrative authority serving Frinton, Great Holland, Kirby and Walton. Occasional reference is made to items just beyond the boundary and for convenience, the southern limit has been taken as Holland Haven, rather than following the strict boundary to Sandy Point. The seaward limit by necessity must be somewhat arbitrary, but generally incidents have been included which would either have been within visual range, of 10 miles or so from the coast, or further out if the Walton & Frinton lifeboat was involved in any way.

The source material has come almost exclusively from the contemporary records of official bodies such as individual units of the Armed Services, the A.R.P. (Air Raid Precautions) organisation, Royal Observer Corps (transcribed by Derek Webb), R.N.L.I., Coastguards, Frinton & Walton Urban District Council etc. Where other sources have been used, they are identified as such in the text. There has been no attempt to make judgements about the events and incidents described, merely to record them. The length of each entry does not necessarily relate to its significance, but after the passage of so many years, it often reflects what it has been possible to discover.

A key document that formed the foundation of this diary was the 'Chart of Air Raid Warnings and Incidents' compiled by Walter Lowther–Kemp, wartime A.R.P. Executive Officer for the area. The time of each air raid warning, from the 'alert' to the 'all clear' was noted for each day of the war and a brief note was added when a particular incident occurred. Many years ago I was able to view this document, the whereabouts of which are unknown today. Although that log formed an excellent starting point, it did only record things of an A.R.P. nature and so there was a long way to go to get at the full story. However that record was a most advantageous start to compiling this diary and I am most grateful to have been able to refer to it.

The late Bill and Florence Candler retained some of the wartime leaflets distributed in Walton and so it has been possible to reproduce them here in a suitable context.

Photography was not an activity encouraged in the wartime coastal defence zone, so few local 'snaps' exist. I am therefore grateful to the Photographic Department of the Imperial War Museum for permitting the reproduction of photographs from their collection and likewise to the library staff of the National Monuments Record. My thanks is also extended to all the others who kindly provided relevant photographic material and who are acknowledged within the text.

Geoff Rayner

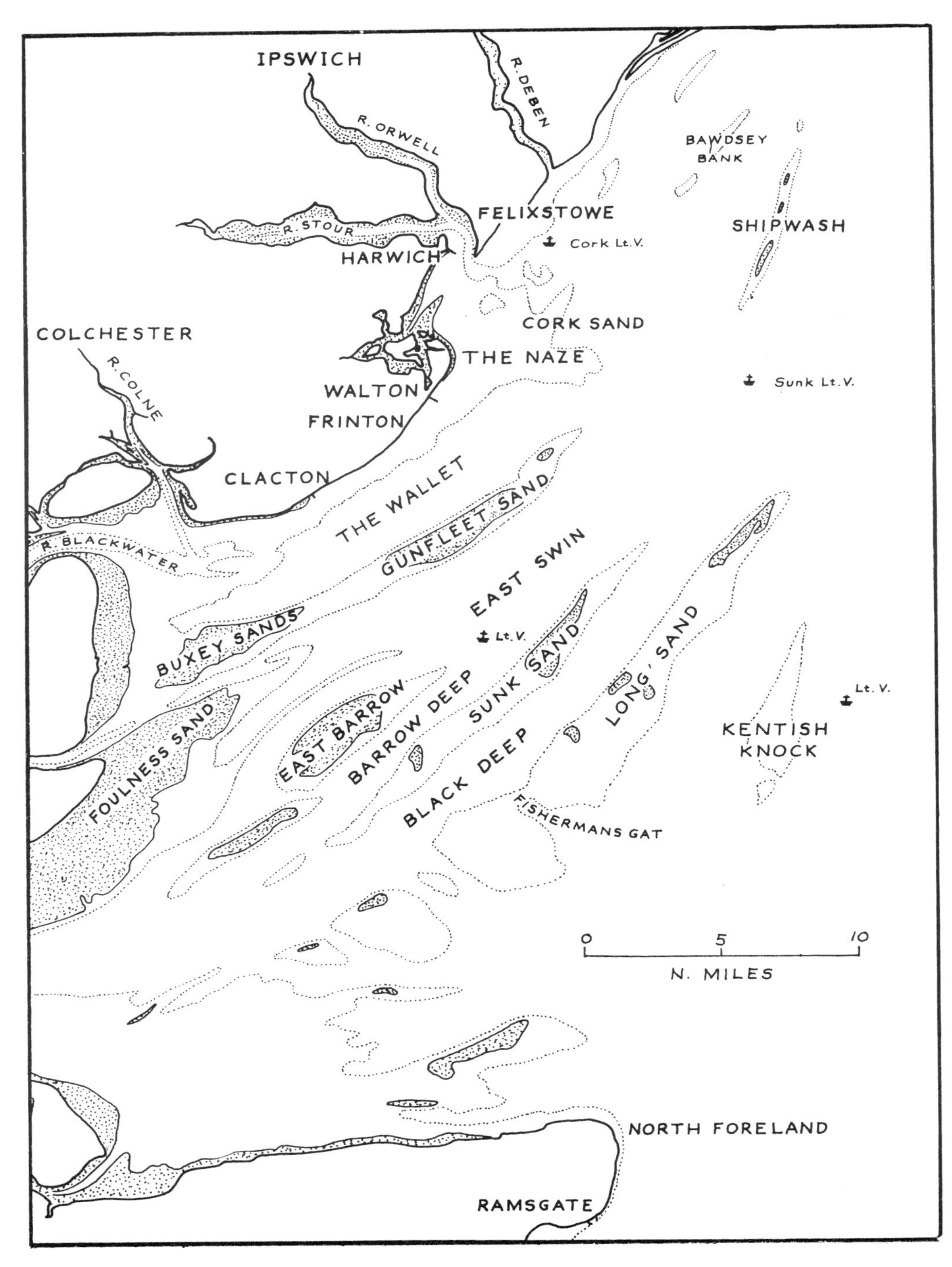

The Thames Estuary

1939

On 17th July 1939, Walton Coastguards reported that an aircraft had crashed in the sea between Walton Pier and the Gunfleet Lighthouse and that the pilot had been seen to come down by parachute. Hurricane L1623 of 87 Squadron, on a routine flight, had developed control problems and Pilot Officer Kenneth Tait had baled out. Both the Walton & Frinton and Clacton lifeboats were launched and, together with Royal Air Force speedboats and aircraft, they conducted a search for the pilot. As it turned out, Pilot Officer Tait was picked up by one of the aircraft, but nevertheless the R.N.L.I. received a letter of thanks from the Royal Air Force in recognition of their services during the rescue.

This was an unusual task for the two lifeboats, but it was the start of what was to become an all too familiar pattern over the following six years.

Kenneth Tait survived that experience but the sea was destined to claim him when two years later he failed to return from a sortie over the North Sea.

Friday, 1 September

Dawn, Hitler's armed forces invaded Poland. Britain responded through its Ambassador in Berlin, who informed the German Government that, unless it ceased hostilities and withdrew its forces, the United Kingdom would be obliged to honour its guarantee of assistance to Poland.

Sunday, 3 September

Just after four in the morning, the Walton Coastguard watchman reported a distress flare about one and a half miles south of Walton Pier. The weather was clear, with a strong breeze making the sea rather rough. The Walton & Frinton lifeboat *E.M.E.D.* was launched at 4.50 and found the barge *Eureka,* of Harwich, with three men on board. Her main sail was damaged and she was completely unmanageable. At her skipper's request, the lifeboatmen boarded the *Eureka* and then took her in tow, arriving at Harwich at 7.35. The lifeboat was back on station at Walton by 10.15 a.m.

It had been a routine operation on what could have been just another Sunday morning, but for the news which came an hour later on the radio. At 11.15 the Prime Minister, Neville Chamberlain, broadcast to the nation from Number 10 Downing Street.

"...This morning the British Ambassador in Berlin handed the German Government a final note, stating that unless we heard from them by 11 o'clock, that they were prepared, at once, to withdraw their troops from Poland, a state of war would exist between us. I have to tell you now, that no such undertaking has been received and that consequently this country is at war with Germany..."

Thus came confirmation of what many had seen as inevitable. Within less than a quarter of a century, Britain was again at war with Germany and Europe was in turmoil.

Monday, 4 September

The first Air Raid Precautions (A.R.P.) 'Red Alert' began at two minutes past three in the morning. Locally there was no apparent enemy activity and the alert was cancelled a quarter of an hour later. Thus occurred the first event to be listed in the logbook of 'Air Raid Warnings and Incidents', compiled by the honorary sub–controller of the local Civil Defence organisation, Councillor Walter Lowther-Kemp.

Tuesday, 3 October

At about 4 p.m. Coastguard watchman Butterfield reported that a motor yacht, lying about two miles 'south–west by south' of Walton Pier, was flying a distress signal: her white ensign upside–down. A moderate easterly gale was blowing and the sea was very rough. The lifeboat *E.M.E.D.* was launched twenty five minutes later and found the motor–yacht *Herga*, of Guernsey, with a crew of six, in difficulties with her engine. At the *Herga's* request the lifeboat began to escort her to Harwich, but not long afterwards it became necessary to take the motor–yacht in tow. After berthing the yacht at Parkeston Quay, the lifeboat returned to Walton just before ten in the evening.

Saturday, 14 October

The sailing barges *Esterel* and *Yampa*, of London, were on their way from London to Norwich with cargoes of maize. When nearly opposite Orfordness they were caught by an easterly gale. Both barges turned back and a while later both struck the Cork Sands off Harwich. The *Esterel* succeeded in getting off. Her sprit was carried away, her sails were in ribbons and the heavy seas stove in her hatches. She was out of control and eventually was driven ashore half a mile north of the Coastguard Station at Walton. The R.N.L.I. report of the incident continues:

"The tide was at half flood. The barge was lying 100 yards from the shore, aground in about six feet of water. She was surrounded by heavy breaking seas, which were smashing the bathing huts on the shore. The coastguard life–saving rocket apparatus was quickly on the scene, and managed to send a line to her, but she swung round, and the line got under her bottom and was useless.

At 9.50 a.m. the Walton & Frinton motor lifeboat *E.M.E.D.* was launched, and a quarter of an hour later she reached the barge. The coxswain anchored to windward and dropped down stern first towards the bow of the barge. When he was off her bow he moved the cable from the forward post of the lifeboat to the starboard after bollard and then steamed in under the lee side of the barge. By this manoeuvre, which brought his cable tight round the barge's bow, he drew the stern of the lifeboat against the barge. Lines were thrown from the lifeboat to the barge, fore and aft, and by keeping the boat still steaming ahead, the coxswain held her long enough alongside for the master, his wife, the mate and the dog to jump aboard her.

Now came the most dangerous moment. The lifeboat was not more than fifty yards from the rocks, and the water was so shallow that she struck the bottom several times. The coxswain dared not risk going any nearer the shore and, with so small a space in which to manoeuvre, it was most difficult and hazardous to get away from the barge. He moved the lifeboat carefully astern, hauling on his cable at the same time, and thus brought her clear of the bows of the barge. Heavy seas were breaking over her the whole time. The slightest mistake would have put her ashore. When the lifeboat, going astern, was far enough from the shore, the coxswain shifted the cable again from the after bollard to the forward post, went ahead on his engines, and picked up his anchor.

The lifeboat arrived back at her station at 11.30, an hour and forty minutes after putting out. As soon as she had landed the rescued she put out again for, fifty minutes before, the coastguard had received from the Cork Light–vessel a signal that a vessel was in distress. The honorary secretary of the station, Captain William J.Oxley, went out with her. There was a very big swell running, with a confused sea, and the gale was blowing fresh from the north–east.

The coxswain made straight for the Cork Sands, as he could see a barge ashore there. He reached her in an hour and twenty minutes and found her completely submerged. She was the *Yampa,* the sister barge to the *Esterel,* which had been with her when she put back off Orfordness. Nothing could be seen of her crew. Very heavy seas were running on the sands, and to make certain that no one was in the rigging, the lifeboat made two complete circles of the barge. Then she made a call on the light–vessel, spoke to a mine–sweeper, and searched the Wallet, the channel between the mainland and Gunfleet Sand, for six miles, but she could neither learn nor find anything of the men. Finally, the coxswain spoke to the Walton coastguard, but they had no information to give. It was clear that the men were drowned, and the lifeboat returned to Walton arriving at three in the afternoon.

The rescue of the crew of the *Esterel* was a very fine service, carried out under very difficult conditions, and it was only through the great skill and fine seamanship of Coxswain T. H. Bloom that the crew were rescued and the lifeboat brought out again from her perilous position practically undamaged. The coxswain's manoeuvre in shifting his cable was a clever idea very skilfully carried out. The assistant motor mechanic, F. Bacon, who was in charge of the engines in the absence of the motor mechanic, managed them very skilfully, and the signalman, F. Williams, kept in touch with the coastguard throughout the rescue by means of the searchlight, a very difficult thing to do in the heavy seas."

Walton & Frinton Lifeboat *E.M.E.D.* and crew involved in the *Esterel* and *Yampa* incident on 14th October 1939.
via Walton Maritime Museum.

After the storm was over; the *Esterel* beached at Walton. Two days later she was salvaged by Harwich shrimpers and towed to Harwich.
Marjorie Norman

After the *Esterel* rescue the R.N.L.I. made the following awards [the numbers refer to the photograph opposite]:
To Coxswain T. H. Bloom, (1) the silver medal for gallantry, and a copy of the vote inscribed on vellum;
To Second Coxswain Walter J. Oxley, (2) the bronze medal for gallantry, and a copy of the vote inscribed on vellum;
To F. Bacon, (3) the assistant motor mechanic, the bronze medal for gallantry, and a copy of the vote inscribed on vellum;
To F. Williams, (4) the boat signalman, the bronze medal for gallantry, and a copy of the vote inscribed on vellum;
To each of the other five members of the crew, E. Oxley (5), A. Halls (6), G. Aldrich (7), A. E. Cook (8) and G. Sharman (9), the thanks of the Institution inscribed on vellum.
[Captain W. J. Oxley (10) was the honorary secretary of the lifeboat.]

Saturday, 28 October

In the morning a gale was blowing and at ten past eleven North Foreland Radio reported via Ramsgate Coastguards, that a radio distress message had been received from the Dutch motor vessel *Pegasus,* that she was sinking in heavy seas in the vicinity of the South Shipwash Buoy (11 miles east–north–east of Walton). The lifeboat was launched and proceeded to assist, but before arriving another vessel managed to take off six of the crew and the danger was over. The Captain and Second Engineer remained on board *Pegasus* and the vessel anchored S.W. Gunfleet. The lifeboat returned, her services no longer required.

November

There had now been two months of what was to become known as the 'phoney war' and for many areas of Britain that was to remain the case for many months to come. Sporadic confrontation had taken place in the air and at sea away from the shores of Britain, but in November the menace of the magnetic mine brought the war that much closer to the shores of eastern England and especially to the Thames Estuary. The mines could be laid from surface craft such as small fast 'E Boats', or by parachute from aircraft, utilising the standard Heinkel He111 bomber or the Heinkel He115 floatplane.

Conventional sea mines relied on impact with a vessel for detonation, but magnetic mines could be triggered merely by the proximity of a ship's steel hull, making them much more potent weapons. The confined channels of the Thames Estuary were ideal for intercepting coastal shipping and by mid November magnetic mines had begun to exact their toll closer to the Essex shore.

Saturday, 18 November

The 8,300 ton Dutch liner *Simon Bolivar,* on passage from Holland to the Dutch West Indies, struck a magnetic mine and sank 12 miles east of the Naze. The initial explosion caused many casualties. Later it was reported that a second explosion occurred some 15 minutes after the first, believed to have been from another mine. Other vessels were quickly at the scene and over 300 of the 400 passengers and crew were saved. Survivors, many soaked in fuel oil, were landed at Harwich, where they were dispersed to hospitals in the surrounding area.

Tuesday, 21 November

12.52 p.m. At Walton Coastguard Station, Watchman Parsons witnessed an explosion on the horizon due east of the Station. No distress signals were seen, but the lifeboat was despatched immediately. The R.N.L.I. report continues:

"The Japanese steamer *Terukuni Maru*, of Tokyo, bound for London, was sunk by enemy action about one and a half miles east of the NE Gunfleet Buoy. A light easterly breeze was blowing. The sea was calm. At 1.17 p.m. the lifeboat *E.M.E.D.* was launched, and on reaching the sinking steamer found that the passengers and crew had been picked up from their own boats by the Trinity House vessel *Alert.* The lifeboat spoke to the *Alert* and offered her help. As everyone on the steamer had been rescued, and the weather was fine it was not needed. The lifeboat, with other vessels, then searched the neighbourhood for an hour, but found nothing except a ship's boat, which she towed back, reaching her station at 5.40 p.m."

The *Terukuni Maru* sinking during the afternoon of 21st November 1939.

Courtesy of Harwich Maritime Museum

In the same area *S.S. Geraldus* also fell victim to a mine. She sank 8 miles east of Walton, just a mile and a half from where the *Terukuni Maru* had gone down.

Perhaps even more worrying for the Admiralty was the loss that evening of the destroyer *H.M.S. Gipsy,* along with many of her crew, to a mine at the entrance of Harwich Harbour. At that time there was no minesweeping counter measure to magnetic mines and the possibility that a Naval Base might effectively be sealed–off by such weapons was of the utmost concern.

Wednesday, 22 November

The carnage continued in the local area as the *S.S. Lowland,* carrying a cargo of coal, was mined and sank within a mile of where the *S.S. Geraldus* had settled.

There was one piece of good fortune though. That evening an aircraft was seen to drop a 'parachute mine' on to the intertidal flats off Shoeburyness. At the next low tide the object was inspected by a team from the Royal Navy's Mine Warfare Section. Subsequently it was deactivated and the secrets of the magnetic mine revealed. Counter measures, in the form of a method of changing the magnetic signature of all vessels, were put into effect forthwith.

Sunday, 3 December

Late in the afternoon the Walton Coastguard Station received a message from the signal station at Felixstowe, that an unknown sailing barge was in difficulties 1000 yards east of Brackenbury Fort, Felixstowe. The lifeboat was launched and proceeded to the area. Nothing was found in the vicinity and after a search the lifeboat returned at 10.25 p.m., the Coxswain reporting that nothing had been seen of the barge.

Thursday, 14 December

In the early afternoon it was reported that two ships' lifeboats had been seen drifting some 5 miles east–south–east of Walton, by the north end of the Gunfleet Sands. Both the Walton & Frinton and Clacton lifeboats were launched. After a search, no boats were to be seen, but instead, seven large tree trunks some four to five feet in diameter were found. The Hydrographer of the Navy and Trinity House were informed of the danger to shipping and the lifeboats returned to their stations in the early evening.

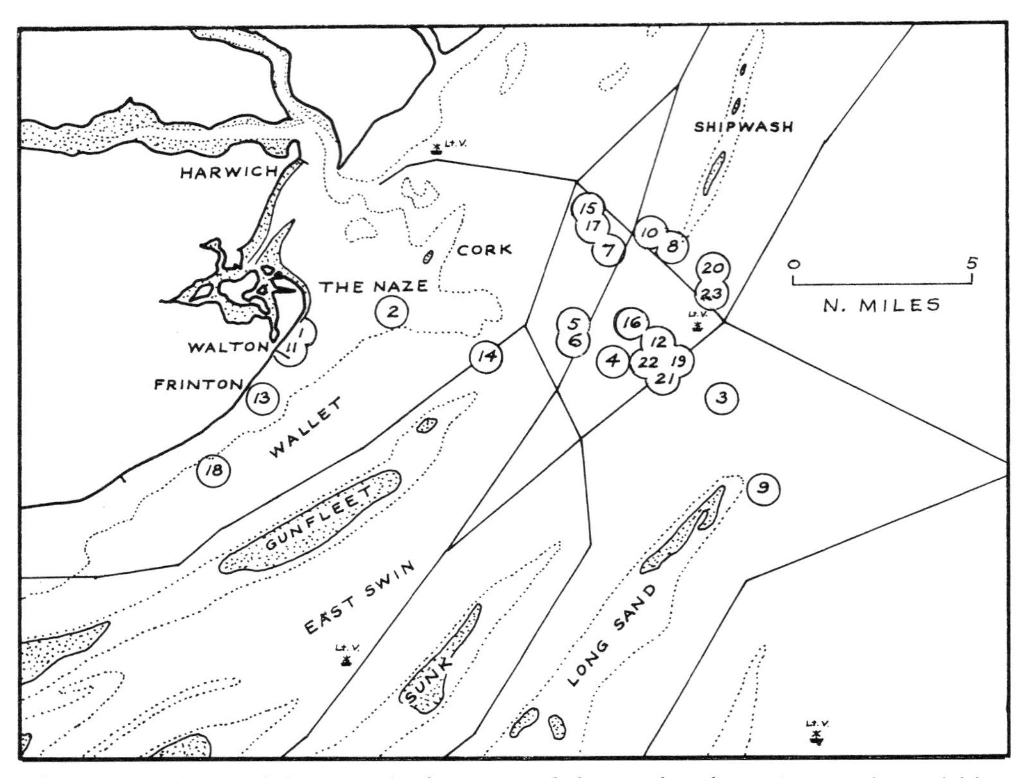

Shipping casualties and the network of recommended routes based on minesweeping activities that developed as the war progressed.

1. Esterel	3 Oct 39	13. Belgia	26 Jan 41
2. Yampa	3 Oct 39	14. Lord St Vincent	7 Jul 41
3. Simon Bolivar	18 Nov 39	15. Marconi	20 Sep 41
4. Terukuni Maru	21 Nov 39	16. Vancouver	21 Sep 41
5. Geraldus	21 Nov 39	17. Norwich Trader	6 Jan 42
6. Lowland	22 Nov 39	18. Resolute	28 Jan 43
7. Protinus	18 Mar 40	19. Dynamo	17 April 43
8. Zbaraz	15 Jul 40	20. Cormorant	13 Nov 43
9. Cape Finisterre	2 Aug 40	21. Morar	27 Nov 43
10. William Wesney	7 Nov 40	22. Norhaur	21 Dec 43
11. Martha	19 Jan 41	23. MMS 227	20 May 44
12. Bonnington Court	19 Jan 41		

1940

Monday, 15 – Tuesday, 16 January

At 9.12 p.m. the naval authorities at Harwich and North Foreland Radio reported that the *S.S. Kildale* had been mined 2 miles east of the Sunk Light–vessel; tugs were being despatched to the area and the immediate launch of the lifeboat was required. There followed a second report that the *Kildal*e had anchored 2 miles east of the Ship Head Buoy (10 miles east of The Naze) and that the captain and crew had returned onboard.

The Lifeboat *E.M.E.D.* launched at 9.50 p.m. and was instructed to call at the Sunk Light–vessel on route for any updated information. (It should be remembered that at this time the prime means of communication for the lifeboat was visually by signal lamp.)

Further reports told of men adrift in one or more boats and the message was relayed to the lifeboat via radio link with the Sunk Light–vessel. The lifeboat remained out all night but the following morning she closed the coast to communicate with the Coastguards, reporting that the *Kildale* was now at anchor near the Cork Light–vessel and asking if any of the missing crew had been found as their search had revealed nothing? The response from the naval authorities at Harwich was that the missing men were believed to have been picked up by another vessel *(Grampian).*

The Lifeboat stood down from the search and returned to her station, reporting as ready for further service at 1.15 p.m. However the day had yet more to offer the lifeboat crew.

Less than a couple of hours later, Frank Oxley, an assistant at the Naze golf course saw a motor barge burning red flares off 'Tamarisk Point', the most northern part of the golf course. He telephoned the Coastguard Station, reporting the flares and that the vessel appeared to be dragging its anchor. A member of the coastguard was sent to the Naze to observe and report, and the Felixstowe Signal Station was asked to keep a lookout. At 4 p.m. the Lifeboat *E.M.E.D.* was away again, but 15 minutes later both Felixstowe and the Naze lookouts reported the motor–barge, '*The Miller*', to be underway and proceeding towards Harwich. The Lifeboat was recalled using signal rocket and signal lamp.

Monday, 29 – Tuesday, 30 January

The weather was very bad. A gale was blowing onshore from east of south–east and visibility was poor. At about 6.30 p.m. in the outer Thames Estuary, 19 miles south–east of Walton, rockets and flares were seen by the Master of the Kentish Knock Light–vessel, 3 miles to the north–east of his vessel. The Walton Coastguard Station was alerted by radio and the message passed to the Naval Flag Officer in Charge at

Harwich, Trinity House and the lifeboat authorities. Permission was given to launch the lifeboat. The R.N.L.I. report continues:

"A fresh east-south-east gale was blowing, with a very rough sea and snow squalls. Two extra men were taken. With great difficulty the crew got aboard the motor life–boat *E.M.E.D.*, which lies at moorings [at the end of Walton Pier], and put out at 7.40 p.m."

One of the measures taken to hamper enemy minelaying operations had been to extinguish the normal navigation lights in the Thames Estuary and to suspend shipping movements during the hours of darkness. Without the use of such aids, navigation in the narrow channels of the Thames Estuary became a hazardous undertaking for friend and foe alike. A request was therefore made for the light–vessel to burn her lantern. The Naval Commander in Chief (C.in C.) Nore, whose area of responsibility covered the Thames Estuary, gave permission for half an hour's exposure between 10.45 and 11.15 p.m.

"They searched until 2 a.m., when they found the *S.S. Highwave*, of London, with her engine broken down. The lifeboat tried to find the lightship, in order to send a wireless message for a tug, but failed, so returned to her station, and passed the request for the tug to the coastguard. It was then ten in the morning, and she had been out for fourteen hours."

In recognition of the time at sea in such arduous conditions, an increase in the usual monetary awards was made to each member of the crew. Additionally, an extra allowance was made to one lifeboatman suffering from frostbite as a result of that night's service.

Later, at just after 5 p.m. on the afternoon of Tuesday 30th January, the Kentish Knock Light–vessel reported that it and a Steamer [*S.S. Highwave?*] were being bombed by an aircraft. Forty minutes later the light–vessel reported that it had survived the attack, but that the steamer had been sunk. A Dutch vessel in the vicinity was believed to have picked up survivors.

Thursday, 1 February

Just before midnight, two mines were washed ashore at the Naze.

Friday, 2 February

In the early afternoon the mines washed ashore at the Naze were reported as exploded. Also a barrage balloon came down on the Naze foreshore.

Sunday, 4 – Monday, 5 February

"At about 7.20 p.m. Walton Coastguards received information from the Kentish Knock Light–vessel that a vessel was sounding S.O.S. on a siren, a few miles west–north–west. A south–west breeze was blowing, there was thick fog, and a very heavy swell on the sands. The motor lifeboat *E.M.E.D.* was launched at 9 p.m."

Permission was obtained for the light–vessel to burn her lantern for a quarter of an hour either side of midnight and she was also asked to use a flashing lamp to help guide the lifeboat.

"She found the motor vessel *Flores,* of Amsterdam bound from Rotterdam to Swansea with pig iron, ashore on the Kentish Knock Sands. She had a crew of seven, but one of them had gone adrift in the ship's boat. Her rudder and steering gear had both been carried away and she was making water. The lifeboat went to the light–vessel and asked her to signal for a tug in a hope of saving the vessel, but the *Flores* signalled her to come back. The lifeboat found that she was making water fast, and took off the six men. It was a difficult rescue in the thick fog and heavy swell, and the lifeboat was slightly damaged. She searched for the missing boat, but without success, and returned to her station at 11.a.m. on 5th February, having been out for fourteen hours. An increase of 10 shillings [50p] in the usual money awards on the standard scale was made to each member of the crew."

Monday, 18 March

The trawler *Protinus* sank after being bombed and machine–gunned by German aircraft approximately 6 miles north–east of the Gunfleet Sands.

Wednesday, 27 March

During the early morning a barrage balloon, adrift from the Harwich anti–aircraft defences, headed south towards the eastern tip of the Naze.

Drifting balloons were a hazard; the steel cable trailing beneath them could cause endless damage if dragged through built up areas, not to mention the snagging of overhead power and telephone lines in open country. For an aircraft at night, friend or foe, the encounter could be catastrophic. The proximity of the Harwich balloon defences meant that rogue balloons were not an uncommon sight, but only some of the escapees are recorded here.

Tuesday, 2 April

Just before midday a message was received at Walton Coastguard Station that a Hurricane aircraft had been reported in distress at a position one mile off the entrance to the River Deben.

Earlier in the morning two Hurricanes from 151 Squadron had taken off from R.A.F. Martlesham Heath, near Ipswich, on a routine Convoy Patrol. 'Blue 1', Flight Lieutenant Ives, had returned at 12.05 p.m. but his No.2, Pilot Officer Fenton, in Hurricane L1799, was missing. Cloud was 'three tenths' at about 4,000 feet and visibility was good except in local showers.

The Lifeboat *E.M.E.D.* was launched and the Naval Authorities at Harwich despatched four M.T.B. Patrol Vessels to the search area. The near–shore and coastline were covered by the regular and auxiliary Coastguards from Felixstowe, Woodbridge

Haven and Shingle Street. Nothing was found. By 6 p.m. the Lifeboat had returned, its search called off. An hour later Walton Coastguards were informed that the aircraft had been located to the north–east of Long Sand Head, some 16 miles south–east of the original position given.

There was no sign of Pilot Officer Fenton and he remains as having 'no known grave'. It is believed that his Hurricane dived into the sea after he lost control in low cloud with insufficient height to recover.

Tuesday, 9 April

Germany invaded Norway and Denmark

Saturday, 20 April

Just after 4 p.m. the Observer Corps reported heavy explosions from offshore at Walton, which were believed to be from a convoy under attack.

Tuesday, 30 April

The stark reality of war arrived abruptly at neighbouring Clacton–on–Sea just before midnight. A Heinkel He111 bomber carrying two sea–mines crashed into a house in Victoria Road in the heart of the town's residential area. The four crew members were killed as well as two civilians: the first civilian casualties in England. One of the mines exploded with devastating effect on surrounding properties. Scores of houses were damaged and over a hundred people were injured. The second mine was recovered intact; inspected, it revealed further secrets of a different variety of magnetic mine.

Friday 10 May 1940

At dawn Germany invaded Holland, Belgium and Luxemburg. Neville Chamberlain resigned. Winston Churchill became Prime Minister and a Coalition Government was formed.

Tuesday 14 May 1940

The German Army broke through the Allied defences on the French border with southern Belgium.

Monday, 20 May

As the situation across the Channel deteriorated, the 15th (Scottish) Division was placed under the Army's Eastern Command and brought south with instructions to take over the defence of Essex by 1200 hours on 26th May.

One of the Division's infantry brigades (45 Brigade) came from the Scottish borders and moved to the Dunmow and Braintree areas. The brigade consisted of three infantry battalions: the 9th and 10th Cameronians and the 6th Royal Scots Fusiliers. Only the two Cameronian battalions came to Essex though, as in April the 6th Royal

Scots Fusiliers had been sent to France to help strengthen the British Expeditionary Force.

Thursday, 24 May

The Commander of 45 Infantry Brigade was given the task of preparing to defend 'Sub–Area No.3', the area of North East Essex lying between the Rivers Stour and Blackwater. The unit's role was to be threefold:
1. To oppose landings on the coast in that sector.
2. To prevent any enemy advance on London
3. Immediate action against inland airborne landings by the use of mobile sub–units.

An assortment of training and support units had been rushed to the coast to help create some form of anti–invasion defence line; these units now came under the brigade's command structure. 45 Brigade thus consisted of:

9th and 10th Battalions, The Cameronians
16/5 Lancers
17/21 Lancers
5th (Training Battalion) Welsh Guards (less rear party)
166 O.C.T.U. (Officer Cadet Training Unit)
4 Training Centre A.M.P.C. (Auxiliary Military Pioneer Corps)
One Squadron (horsed) 4th Cavalry Training Regiment
4th Reserve Anti–Tank Training Regiment
One Troop (4.5 inch Howitzers) 130 Field Regiment, R.A.
280 Field Company
One Signals Section from 36 Signals Training Regiment, R.A.
All Local Defence Volunteers (L.D.V.), later known as the Home Guard.

Although the list appears long, they were meagre resources to cover such a large area. In theory the two main infantry battalions would consist of about 1,000 men each, but there were some 20 miles of coastline to be defended.

The military authorities looked upon the L.D.V. (Home Guard) as a static force whose individual units would be under the operational control of the local sub–area Army Commander. In 45 Brigade's area the L.D.V. was considered to be most usefully employed: providing guards for road blocks, for the destruction of local petrol supplies (if required), the removal or disabling of private cars and the provision of guides for regular troops operating in their localities.

Sunday, 26 May

Evacuation of the British Expeditionary Force began from the port and beaches of Dunkirk, close to the Franco–Belgian border.

In Essex, the Defence of Sub–Area No.3 was being planned as a series of observation posts and road blocks just inland from the coast in a line running from the Maldon area, north–east through Tolleshunt D'Arcy, Peldon to Alresford, then through Great Bentley, Weeley, Great Oakley and Little Oakley. These positions were to be established by the following morning.

The form of attack expected was either by sea–borne troops landing on the coast, by troop carrying aircraft landing on suitable beaches or inland, or by parachute troops inland.

When required, the observation posts would be reinforced to form an 'outpost line' capable of all–round defence. Independent garrisons for local protection were established at Harwich (5th Training Battalion Welsh Guards), Walton & Frinton (4th Reserve Anti–Tank Regiment) and at Clacton (4 Training Centre A.M.P.C.).

To set the tone of the defence plan in no uncertain terms, the 'Operational Instruction' implementing it added: "Whatever the form and whatever the strength of hostile attack, resistance must be to the last. There is to be no withdrawal or evasion. All ranks must clearly understand this cardinal requirement."

Thursday, 30 May

Early in the afternoon the Ministry of Shipping sought the help of the R.N.L.I. in its search for small craft. The Institution immediately contacted eighteen of its stations in south–east England between Gorleston and Shoreham, asking each to send its lifeboat to Dover together with a full crew, full fuel tanks and a towing hawser for, 'special duties under the Admiralty'.

The *E.M.E.D.* was soon on its way. Other Walton lifeboatmen manned a new and as yet unnamed self–righting lifeboat which had just been completed at Rowhedge. (Later this lifeboat was named *Guide of Dunkirk*, reflecting a monetary donation by Girl Guides and the vessel's service at Dunkirk.)

It was not hard to guess what the lifeboats were required for and some if not all the lifeboatmen had expected to remain with their boats for the forthcoming task; after all, they knew the boats better than anyone else, but it was not to be. Apparently there had been a misunderstanding when the first few boats arrived at Dover; Royal Navy crews were assigned and the lifeboatmen were given travel warrants for their journeys home.

The *E.M.E.D.* arrived off Dunkirk the following day, 31st May, under the command of Lieutenant R. Mead RNVR. As with most of the small craft, she had been towed over in a group by tug, thus saving fuel. Her exact movements and accomplishments during the evacuation are not recorded. Lieutenant Mead was killed during the action and at one time the *E.M.E.D.* was found with a fouled propeller and was towed back to Dover where she landed thirty nine men. Divers freed the rope and she returned to Dunkirk.

The lifeboat was not the only local boat to be called upon for service at the evacuation. Sometime before 'Dunkirk', the Admiralty had begun a register of smaller craft for its possible future use and so a pool of known vessels already existed.

Mr D. Bostock, a former Commodore of the Walton & Frinton Yacht Club between 1933 and 1937, ran a boat building and motor engineering business at the end of Walton's Mill Lane. Two of the vessels built there were *Singapore* (in 1934), a 32 foot motor yacht and *Singapore II* (in 1937), a 32 foot motor cruiser.

Both boats took part in the Dunkirk evacuation and what little is known about each vessels' involvement is related in Christian Brann's *The Little Ships of Dunkirk* (Collectors' Books): *Singapore* was commanded by Lieutenant J.W. Pratt RNVR and *Singapore II* was commanded by Sub Lieutenant F.E. Greenfell RN. *Singapore* ran aground on the Dunkirk beaches on 2nd June, but was refloated on the next tide. On the return journey she took in tow three lifeboats, but then broke down and was herself towed back. Both boats still survive today and are registered with the 'Association of Dunkirk Little Ships'.

Two of Walton's small craft that took part in the Dunkirk evaculation.

Left, *Singapore* in Piraeus, Greece, a few years ago.

Below, *Singapore II* re-enacts the trip to Dunkirk at a gathering of the Association of Dunkirk Little Ships.

Collectors' Books

A further reminder of the conflict came later in the afternoon with the sudden arrival of two Spitfires which made forced landings in Frinton and Walton.

A few days previously No.609 (West Riding) Squadron, Royal Auxiliary Air Force, had been brought south to R.A.F. Northolt on the western outskirts of London, to help cover the evacuation across the Channel. May 30th saw the Squadron's first operational sortie over the beaches of Dunkirk.

The Spitfires were returning in poor weather and very low on fuel. For some the fuel state turned critical as they approached the north Essex coast, a long way from their direct route back to Northolt. Flying Officer Frank Howell, flying Spitfire N3203, later described his experience in a letter to his brother.

"After one hour, we returned home but all over the coast a lovely sea mist had appeared and of course, like a bloody fool I got lost, or rather I missed the tip of Kent and hit the coast right up south of Harwich! We could see just about F all and had only 10 gallons of petrol left. I went down to read the name of a station and found it to be Walton–on–the–Naze. That conveyed as much to me as Slopton–on–the–Mud, so it became highly obvious that unless I landed during the next ten minutes, nature would take its course and gravity would bring me down for I certainly would not have any petrol.

Of the two blokes I was with, one knew where he was and reached an aerodrome 30 miles away, the other cheerily called me up on the R/T and said he was quite all right and had landed in a cricket field – that left me!

There was quite a nice golf club on the cliffs near the sea so I thought that was the nearest place to a drink so looked out for a fairway with no bunkers. There was a beauty, but with three people playing on it – at least they did not play, but watched me. I flew low and slowly over them, waving my hand for them to get out of the light, but all they did was to smile and wave stupidly back. Petrol getting lower! So I had to choose a much more crooked one further down and by nearly killing a dozen sheep, managed to put it down with a perfect three point landing (ahem!) and with no damage! Whew.

The story really ends there, for I got some more petrol from an aerodrome and after a crazy take off from a tee, over a couple of fairways, between three bunkers and straight over the cliff, I managed to get back."

His colleague on the cricket pitch was Flying Officer John Dundas. He had landed in the confines of the playing fields between Frinton and Walton. Space there was limited and having safely touched down, Spitfire L1063, ran on into a fence at the far end, ending up on its nose against some iron railings. The pilot was not hurt, but one of the Spitfire's wings was damaged.

Unlike Frank Howell, John Dundas had no choice but to stay awhile. Taken to the Police Station, there Special Constable Sidney Bocking remembers sharing his sandwiches and a mug of tea with the young Flying Officer who, during the subsequent weeks of the Battle of Britain, was to become one of the R.A.F's. top scoring fighter pilots and was awarded the DFC and Bar. He was eventually shot down and killed in November 1940 at the age of 24.

Another member of the squadron, Flying Officer Desmond Ayre, had also made landfall on the north Essex coast. He was not so fortunate. Very low on fuel, it is believed his Spitfire, L1086, spun in to the ground as he attempted a forced landing in the vicinity of the explosives works at Great Oakley. He died on the way to hospital.

Jennifer Dexter

Unexpected visitors.
On 30th May 1940, two Spitfires from 609 Squadron, Royal Auxiliary Air Force, made forced-landings at Walton and Frinton.

Above: F/O Frank Howell in his Spitfire, named FOO. Four victory symbols are painted beneath the windscreen.

Left: F/O John Dundas (left) talking to ground staff at R.A.F. Northolt, June 1940.

via Chris Goss

Saturday, 1 June

A reappraisal of the invasion threat led to a revised defence organisation by 15th (Scottish) Division. The threat was now seen as:

a. In the first instance a landing on suitable beaches by means of troops carried in fast motor boats.
b. If successful, the landing might be followed by attempts to land tanks.
c. Attacks on the coast would be accompanied by strong air action.
d. Attempts to land airborne troops.

45 Brigade subsequently altered its previous plan to one of beach defence. Posts were to be capable of all round defence, with additional all round defence at Clacton, Walton and Harwich. The Brigade HQ, together with the reserve infantry battalion (10th Cameronians), moved from Great Leighs to Wivenhoe Park. The 9th Cameronians were already deployed in the Tollesbury– Goldhanger–Heybridge area.

Monday, 3 June

The final day of the evacuation from Dunkirk.

Tuesday, 4 June

As more troops became available to man the coastal strip, the defence organisation was modified further. No.3 sub–area was divided in two, the dividing line being the road between Nayland and Colchester then south along the River Colne. West of the line became the new Sub–Area No.3a and east of it retained the designation Sub–Area No.3, still the responsibility of the 45th Infantry Brigade's Commander at Wivenhoe Park.

The two Regular Army 'front line' infantry battalions were redeployed. The 9th Cameronians moved into the new sub–area and took up positions at St. Osyth, while the 10th Cameronians moved to Harwich and Dovercourt to relieve the 5th Training Battalion, Welsh Guards. Between the two Cameronian battalions remained the ancillary units which had been rushed to the coast some weeks earlier as a stop gap measure. Beach defence along the Frinton and Walton coastline continued to be the responsibility of the 4th Reserve Anti–Tank Regiment.

In June 1940 the air raid siren sounded six times in response to the 'red alert' status of impending air attack. Before June there had been no red alerts since 1939: two in September and one each in October and November. In July 1940 there were to be seven, but thereafter and for the next year the rate went up dramatically to one or more a day.

Wednesday, 19 June

Considerable enemy activity took place over East Anglia during the night of June 18th and 19th. Aircraft from a number of R.A.F. Squadrons were despatched into the darkness to intercept the various raiders. Navigating at night provided its own complications, especially for single seater aircraft, and the added role of the 'night–fighter' was an art still in its infancy. At that time airborne radar was only just being introduced and there remained a heavy reliance on basic visual contact in whatever gloom the night offered. The network of searchlights could catch an enemy aircraft, but just as easily illuminate a friendly fighter. If the anti–aircraft guns were at action stations, recognition from the ground had to be good.

Just after 1 a.m. the aerial activity brought the Harwich harbour anti–aircraft defences into action. One aircraft was reported down in the sea just off Landguard Point, but in the reporting that followed doubt set in as to whether it was a friendly or enemy machine. The immediate consensus remained that it was an enemy aircraft. Later the body of Pilot Officer John Barnwell was washed up on the beach at Walton–on–the–Naze. His 29 Squadron Blenheim was one of the night–fighter force despatched from R.A.F. Debden that night which had not returned.

Thursday, 27 June

The 6th Battalion King's Own Scottish Borderers joined 45 Brigade and moved forward to augment the beach defence force. The battalion took over the section of coastline from the southern end of Frinton, through Holland–on–Sea, to Clacton. Frinton and Walton remained the responsibility of the 4th Reserve Anti–Tank Regiment.

Monday, 1 July

In the late afternoon a barrage balloon was adrift high over the Naze heading out to sea.

Wednesday, 3 July

The first bombs fell inside the Frinton & Walton Urban District boundary this day. At 3.43 p.m. the Lower Kirby searchlight post reported bombs to the north of Horsey Island, but an hour later 27 high–explosive bombs fell on the Frinton golf course, one of which remained unexploded.

Just before midnight, high–explosive and incendiary bombs set fire to Brooks Mill at Mistley. The Frinton & Walton A.R.P. Rescue Party was sent to give assistance.

Thursday, 4 July

A much travelled 6th Battalion Royal Scots Fusiliers arrived to take over beach defence duties at Frinton and Walton from the 4th Reserve Anti–Tank Regiment, which then took on the sole task of manning the '2 pounder' anti–tank guns along that stretch of coast.

The Royal Scots Fusiliers were returning to 45 Brigade (and 15th (Scottish) Division) after a detached period with 152 Brigade (of the 51st Highland Division), during which time they had seen action in France. The battalion had been based in the Metz area near the Franco–German border and thus found itself to the south of the main German advance through southern Belgium.

Ten days after the fighting began, the 51st (Highland) Division was withdrawn to a reserve position and the men of the 6th Battalion Royal Scots Fusiliers found themselves on the move westward to Rouen and then, by June 1st, to Le Tréport just to the north of Dieppe on the Channel coast. The Division was taking up defensive positions in the Dieppe area in preparation for a further drive westwards by the Germans once the Dunkirk sector had been cleared.

A week later the battalion was on the move again, westwards to Le Havre where the men were transferred by ship further west to Cherbourg. They disembarked but there was uncertainty over their next move. Two days later they were back on board a ship at Cherbourg and sailing for Southampton, where they arrived on June 16th. The following day they arrived 'home' in the Scottish Borders.

Their stay was not long though, as they were required elsewhere. After just two weeks back in the Borders and after each man had been granted a weekend's leave, the battalion was instructed to rejoin the 15th (Scottish) Division's 45 Brigade on the Essex coast, and so the battalion arrived at Frinton and Walton. While attached to the Highland Division the Fusiliers had been a Pioneer Battalion, but once back with 45 Brigade they reverted to a standard front line infantry Field Force unit.

At first they took over the defences from near the Naze Tower through to the Frinton Golf Club, but that was soon modified to the Frinton and Holland shore (from the end of Pole Barn Lane to Holland Haven) in response to other troop redeployments taking place further along the coast. The 4th Reserve Anti–Tank Regiment again became responsible for beach defence at Walton, in addition to manning the anti–tank guns in Frinton as well.

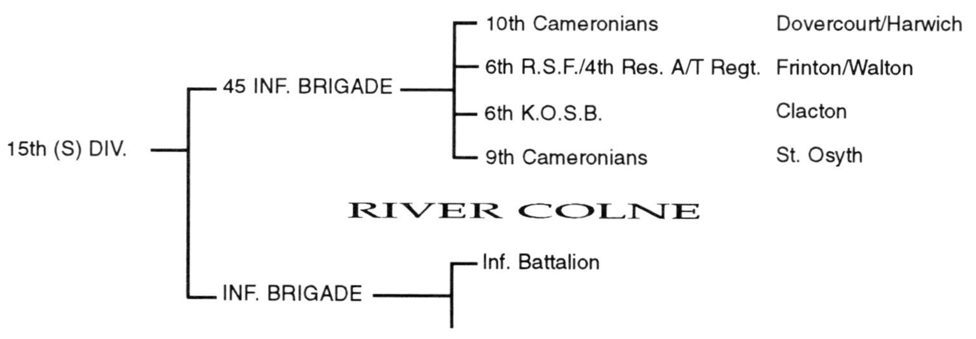

Disposition of Army units along the N.E. Essex coast, early July 1940.

IMPORTANT NOTICE

EVACUATION

The public throughout the country generally are being told to " stay put " in the event of invasion. For military reasons, however, it will in the event of attack be necessary to remove from this town all except those persons who have been specially instructed to stay. An order for the compulsory evacuation of this town will be given when in the judgment of the Government it is necessary, and plans have been arranged to give effect to such an order when it is made.

You will wish to know how you can help NOW in these plans.

THOSE WHO ARE ENGAGED IN WORK OF ANY DESCRIPTION IN THE TOWN SHOULD STAY FOR THE PRESENT.

OTHER PERSONS SHOULD, SO FAR AS THEY ARE ABLE TO DO SO, MAKE ARRANGEMENTS TO LEAVE THE TOWN—PARTICULARLY

MOTHERS WITH YOUNG CHILDREN
SCHOOL CHILDREN
AGED AND INFIRM PERSONS
PERSONS WITHOUT OCCUPATION OR IN RETIREMENT.

All such persons who can arrange for their accommodation with relatives or friends in some other part of the country should do so. Assistance for railway fares and accommodation will be given to those who require it.

Advice and, where possible, assistance will be given to persons who desire to leave the town but are unable to make their own arrangements.

Information about these matters can be obtained from the local Council Offices.

(*Signed*) WILL SPENS,
Regional Commissioner for Civil Defence.

CAMBRIDGE,
2nd July, 1940.

(393/4177) Wt. 19544-30 125M 7/40 H & S Ltd. **Gp. 393**

Waiting for the unknown. A '2 pounder' anti-tank gun on the cliff top at Frinton, July 1940. Walton Pier is on the horizon, above the gun. *I. W. M. H2337*

Juggling units' areas of responsibility was to continue as more front line units became available to supplement and relieve the training and support units despatched to the coast in haste. The 4th Reserve Anti–Tank Regiment was soon to leave the area and then the 6th Battalion, Royal Scots Fusiliers became responsible for the whole of Frinton and Walton.

By this time the construction of defensive works along the shoreline was gathering pace. Barbed wire lined the beaches from Holland Haven through to the low cliffs at the Naze golf course (although in some cases it was only one line deep). Beach mines were about to be laid on areas of low cliff at the southern end of Frinton, to the north of the Walton Coastguard Station and at the northern end of the Naze golf course. Concrete pillboxes had been constructed every few hundred yards along the shore or cliff top. It had been decided that camouflage should take the form of deception rather than concealment and so the pillboxes became bathing huts and other typical seaside structures.

Opposite the Grand Hotel, an addition to the Frinton Greensward was an emplacement for a battery of two 6–inch naval guns. Their arc of fire linked with a similar battery on the Holland–on–Sea cliffs to the right and the large Harwich guns to the left. Field artillery guns were in place further back from the shore line.

Friday, 5 July

At 6.50 a.m. an aircraft machine–gunned the Shipwash Light–vessel. A few minutes later bomb explosions were reported in the same vicinity.

Monday, 8 July

In the early hours of the morning an R.A.F. Hampden bomber crashed by the side of the Great Holland to Clacton road. The previous evening Hampden L4066 of 83 Squadron had taken off from R.A.F. Scampton in Lincolnshire, on a sortie to Frankfurt. Just before 3 a.m. the Hampden crashed at Great Holland, by the main road between Holland Brook and Great Holland Lodge. Three of the crew were dead: Pilot Officer Oliver Launders and Sergeants Basil Kinton and Cyril Hallett. The fourth crew member, Sergeant Leonard Howard survived the crash and was removed to hospital, but he died later. Royal Engineers from the nearby searchlight post at Holland Haven mounted guard on the aircraft wreck until relieved by a Royal Air Force detachment from R.A.F. Martlesham Heath.

At 7.40 p.m. three high–explosive bombs, three unexploded, landed on Horsey Island.

Monday, 15 July

The Polish vessel *S.S. Zbaraz* was bombed and sunk by German aircraft at South Ship Head, 10 miles east–north–east of the Naze.

Thursday, 18 July

At 3.48 p.m. Walton Coastguards received a 'Mayday' signal from the Sunk Light–vessel, 11 miles to the east of Walton, that it had been attacked by enemy aircraft. Trinity House was informed and the Trinity House Tender *Strathearn,* which was already at sea with another light–vessel in tow, was ordered to investigate. At the request of the naval authorities at Harwich the lifeboat was launched, but it turned out that her services were not required. The *Strathearn* exchanged light–vessels and then took the Sunk Light–vessel in tow.

Friday, 19 July

'Movietone News' came to Frinton to film firing of the coastal gun battery opposite the Grand Hotel. Manning of the two 6–inch naval guns had just been transferred from a naval detachment to men of the Royal Artillery.

Saturday, 20 July

At 2.30 a.m. the Observer Corps reported an aircraft in the sea off the Sunk Light–vessel, possibly an enemy seaplane.

The big guns open fire. On 19th July 1940 Movietone News cameras recorded the firing of the two 6-inch ex-naval guns installed on the Frinton cliff top opposite the Grand Hotel.
I. W. M. H2333

Thursday, 25 July

The lifeboat's mooring at the end of the pier had been made inaccessible by the demolition of two sections as an anti invasion measure. Since the lifeboat's return from the Dunkirk operation it had been moored in the Backwaters.

Just before midnight cries for help were heard coming from the direction of Walton Channel in the Backwaters. The Coastguards were informed and the lifeboat was sent to investigate. Hailing the Patrol Boat *Paulette,* it was learned that a dinghy returning to the Patrol Boat with four of the its crew onboard, had capsized. A search was conducted until the *Paulette* reported that all the men were safe onboard.

The Naval Auxiliary Patrol Service had only recently been formed, to patrol the inshore coastal waters. It used requisitioned small craft manned by local men who would be familiar with their own coastal waters.

Wednesday, 31 July

The Royal Scots Fusiliers Commanding Officer had a meeting with the Chairman of the District Council, during which the Council Chairman explained the crumbling nature of the cliffs and stressed the danger of having heavy pillboxes so close to the cliff edge.

For the cameras: men of the 6th Battalion Royal Scots Fusiliers advance on the cliff top at Frinton. The 6-inch gun battery, opposite the Grand Hotel, is to the right of the picture. 19th July 1940. *I. W. M. H2341*

Friday, 2 August

During the night of August 1st and 2nd, an enemy seaplane was fired on by soldiers at the Naze golf course searchlight site, as it flew at low altitude along the coast from the Naze towards Frinton. The only weapons available to the searchlight crew were small arms and light machine–guns. The seaplane flew on a course frequently followed, continuing past Frinton and on beyond St Osyth.

At 7.30 in the evening Walton Coastguards received a radio message from the Sunk Light–vessel that H.M. Trawler *Cape Finisterre* had just been bombed and was foundering 5 miles south– south–east. The lifeboat was launched and on arriving at the scene the Coxswain was told by H.M. Trawler *Regeis* that the *Cape Finisterre* had sunk. The crew, including several casualties, some serious, had been rescued and were being taken to Harwich by a patrol vessel. The lifeboat returned to its station and was ready for service again at 7.30 the next morning.

Saturday, 10 August

Just after midnight bombs fell in the sea south of the searchlight site at Burnt House Farm, Walton.

Further enemy aircraft activity was reported at 10.40 p.m. when the searchlight site at the Naze illuminated a seaplane travelling south–west towards Frinton.

Sunday, 11 August

The period known as the 'Battle of Britain' was well underway and during this particular phase of the aerial confrontation, coastal convoys were a favoured target of the Luftwaffe.

At midday a convoy codenamed 'Booty' came under attack from enemy aircraft when it was some 12 miles east of Clacton. In the ensuing engagement a number of aircraft from both sides were shot down and fell in the sea.

At 12.22 p.m. Walton Coastguards received the message of an aircraft down in the vicinity of the NE Gunfleet. Later reports mentioned a pilot floating in the sea 14 miles off Walton and an aircraft down on Bawdsey Bank, 5 miles off Shingle Street.

The lifeboat was launched at 12.50 p.m. During the search, the Coxswain spoke to the crews of a couple of light–vessels, neither of which had seen any aircraft or wreckage but destroyers had been seen in the vicinity. Finding nothing, the lifeboat returned to Walton.

It is likely that the pilot sought by the lifeboat was Sergeant R.D. Baker from 56 Squadron. The Squadron's Diary of Operations at the time recorded how he had taken off from Rochford [now Southend Airport] for a convoy patrol in Hurricane N2667 and, "was seen to go down and bale out, having apparently been attacked by a lone Spitfire. He was picked up by a destroyer, but was already dead." Two other Spitfires came down further out in the Thames Estuary, neither pilot surviving.

Thursday, 15 August

As the air offensive intensified, the Luftwaffe began to concentrate on Fighter Command's airfields. That Thursday afternoon it was the turn of R.A.F. Martlesham Heath, an airfield on the outskirts of Ipswich being used as a forward base for fighter aircraft. The attack by Messerschmitt Me110's from a specialist unit, came in low and fast just after 3 p.m.

R.A.F. fighters were unable to prevent the attack but afterwards at least two squadrons of Hurricanes became embroiled in a combat with the raiders and their fighter escort, out to sea off Harwich and the Naze.

At Walton the siren had sounded at five minutes past three. From the shore a number of aircraft were seen to fall into the sea, but the exact number was uncertain. One was reported by the A.R.P. as going in between Dovercourt and Walton and was probably the same as that seen and reported by the Coastguards 3 miles north east of their lookout, the pilot coming down by parachute 4 miles east of Walton.

The lifeboat was launched and three M.T.Bs. were despatched by the naval authorities at Harwich, to search for the downed aircraft and their pilots. The lifeboat was out for nearly six hours but without success. Wreckage from a Hurricane was found by a shrimper and two pilots were eventually picked up by other craft, but two RAF pilots remained unaccounted for.

One of the survivors was Flying Officer Douglas Grice of 32 Squadron. He had been flying as his squadron's 'tail–end Charlie', a little above and behind the other aircraft, weaving from side to side to protect the rear of their formation. He recalls that without having sighted the enemy, the squadron turned and was flying south when suddenly –

"I saw something flash over my left wrist into the instrument panel, beyond which was the gravity tank containing 30 gallons of 100 octane fuel. The incendiary bullet did its work and I was then enveloped in flames. They say that there are two sorts of fighter pilot, 'the quick and the dead'. Well I was one of the former and no one could have baled out quicker than I did. Floating down in my parachute, from about 15,000 feet, I was relieved to see the coastline between my feet, but a few minutes later I realised there was an offshore breeze and that I was destined for a splash–down. Once in the water the first thing I saw was a fishing trawler with the crew waving to me, but otherwise steaming straight on. They could see what I could not, namely the M.T.B. approaching at high speed."

In just a few minutes Flying Officer Grice was onboard the M.T.B. and heading towards Harwich Harbour where he was admitted to the Royal Naval Hospital at Shotley for treatment to burns on his face and wrists.

He was fortunate and considers he owes a great debt of gratitude to the naval surgeon who attended him. After being transferred to a London hospital he was seen for assessment by the famous plastic surgeon Archie McIndoe. He remembers at the first meeting McIndoe commenting, in his jocular way, 'I'm afraid I am going to need a piece of your bottom', which was the surgeon's way of saying that skin grafting would be necessary.

However, at the second visit, McIndoe was sufficiently impressed with the way the healing was progressing to announce that Flying Officer Grice would 'look handsome again' without any help from him, as all the right things had been done; adding that, 'we doctors have discovered through you and others that the best immediate treatment for a bad burns case is a brine bath, which you had very quickly'.

In the event the facial burns have quite disappeared and the vindication of McIndoe's prophecy is that today people look doubtingly when Douglas Grice says that in 1940 he had to grow a new face.

F/O Douglas Grice and the 32 Squadron Hurricane, N2459 coded GZ-C, he was forced to abandon on 15th August 1940, just offshore of The Naze. *I. W. M.*

After 32 Squadron lost their 'tail–end Charlie', the remaining aircraft continued the fight further out to sea without further loss, or almost so. A Polish pilot on the squadron, Pilot Officer Wlasnowolski, claimed a Messerschmitt Me109 shot down in flames, but his own aircraft was damaged and he had to force land once back over the Essex coast.

Another R.A.F. squadron involved was No.1 Squadron, whose nine Hurricanes were led by a Canadian, Flight Lieutenant M.H. Brown. His particular section of three aircraft were all shot down. He baled out over the sea, was picked up by a trawler and was landed at Harwich having sustained injuries to his face and hands. Nothing was found of his two colleagues from Red Section, Pilot Officer D.O.M. Browne and Sergeant M.M. Shannon and they remain listed as casualties with no known grave. Other pilots from No.1 Squadron claimed two Messerschmitt Me109's as shot down and seen to fall into the sea.

Sunday, 18 August

Heavy raids on Fighter Command's airfields continued throughout the day. In the late afternoon, two large formations of bombers inbound via the Thames Estuary were intercepted by a strong force of R.A.F. fighters. Numerous individual and group engagements ensued. The local siren sounded the alert at 5.25 p.m., just as one engagement involving 20 R.A.F. fighters and 50 enemy aircraft was observed from the shore at Frinton and Walton. One of the enemy aircraft, a Messerschmitt Me110, crashed at Clacton; the crew did not survive.

Monday, 19 August

At six minutes past midnight and without warning, between 11 and 15 high–explosive bombs and two incendiary bombs fell on the Naze golf course, close to the searchlight site. Just a few minutes later two incendiary bombs fell on the Frinton golf course. Five incendiary bombs were also reported at Kirby and others fell outside the District. Two of the Walton bombs were of the delayed action type and exploded four hours later.

There can be no real doubt that such apparently random bombing was the result of night raiders returning home and dumping any remaining bomb load before heading back over the sea. It was not possible to predict such attacks by single or small groups of aircraft and prior warning was not really possible.

In a series of recommendations on local defence, the Commanding Officer of the local infantry battalion suggested that the Naze Tower should be demolished as it formed a good landmark and thus could assist enemy operations.

Monday, 26 August

Air raid warnings were now virtually a daily occurrence, often several in one day. At 3.10 p.m. the siren sounded as a large raid had been detected inbound over the Thames

Estuary. It passed by to seaward of the District and headed for the R.A.F. airfields further inland in Essex. The 'all clear' was at 4.30 p.m., but half an hour later the siren sounded again. This time the danger was realised as ten minutes later three high–explosive bombs fell on Stone Point at the Naze.

Wednesday, 28 August

At 10.20 p.m. six incendiary bombs fell at Great Holland. Forty minutes later the searchlight sites at Frinton and Clacton reported that an aircraft had exploded in mid–air and had fallen into the sea.

Saturday, 31 August

Without warning, seven high–explosive bombs fell on the Naze golf course at 4.35 a.m.

At 8.05 a.m. the siren sounded as formations of enemy aircraft were approaching the outer Thames Estuary. Before reaching the north Essex coast the raiders turned inland over the Blackwater Estuary, then on towards the north–west and Fighter Command's airfields at Debden and Duxford close to the Essex–Cambridge border. For R.A.F. Debden it was a repeat performance of the raid the previous Monday and again the airfield was badly damaged. R.A.F. Duxford escaped damage as the bombers flew wide of their mark and dropped most of their bomb load on open ground. Released of their burden the enemy bombers turned for home. Several R.A.F. Squadrons had been scrambled to intercept, and as the raiders headed for the coast the fighters made contact. Skirmishes developed over a wide swathe of the Essex countryside and a number of aircraft fell.

No.257 Squadron, then based at R.A.F. Martlesham Heath, had scrambled nine Hurricanes. They saw one enemy formation over the Colchester area, heading out to sea over the Colne and Blackwater Estuaries. They gave chase, but being unable to overhaul the bombers, turned their attention on the escorting Messerschmitt Me110 fighters. Once the initial attack had been made, the fight broke up into a series of individual engagements covering a large area of coastal Essex.

Just before 9 a.m., observers on the ground at the Naze saw, high up, one aircraft being attacked from behind by another; a short burst and the first began to fall. The stricken plane dived towards the ground but at about 5,000 feet came out of its dive, only then to go completely out of control. At 400 feet, and far too low, the pilot baled out. At such a height it left little chance for the parachute to take effect.

From the town it could be seen that the aircraft would come down somewhere over the Backwaters or Pennyhole Bay and so the lifeboat was launched. Later it was recalled when the body of Pilot Officer Gerard Maffett was found on the sand by the Tamarisk seawall at the northern end of the Naze golf course, just yards from the wreckage of his Hurricane. He was 24 years old. He had been a pre–war Volunteer Reserve pilot and had been with 257 Squadron for just eight weeks. This had been his fifth and final combat.

Pilot Officer Gerard Hamilton Maffett.

Geoff Hunt's painting of Pilot Officer Maffett's 257 Squadron Hurricane which fell at The Naze on 31st August 1940.

The remains of Gerard Maffett's Hurricane, P3175 (coded DT–S), were recovered in 1973 and now lie preserved in the Battle of Britain Hall of the RAF Museum at Hendon, London, in the form of a memorial to 'The Few'. The wreckage is the largest single section of any RAF fighter from the Battle of Britain to have been recovered post war. The full story of the raid that morning and the subsequent recovery and preservation of Gerard Maffett's Hurricane is told by the author in "One Hurricane One Raid" (Airlife 1990).

Wednesday, 4 September

Just after 9 p.m. an aircraft was illuminated by the searchlight at Burnt House Farm, Walton and two high–explosive bombs were reported as falling into the sea 4 miles north–east of the site. An air raid alert began twenty minutes later and lasted until midnight, but without any further aerial activity.

Thursday, 5 September

At 5 a.m. an explosion was caused by dogs setting off defence land mines.

Friday, 6 September

At 9.45 a.m., 15 minutes after the air raid siren had sounded, the A.R.P. logged 'parachutists and crashed aircraft', but nothing more. The 'all clear' was sounded after an hour with no further activity.

Saturday, 7 September

The military authorities were on the highest state of alert and the codeword *Cromwell*, indicating invasion imminent, was passed to the Home Forces. Although the invasion did not materialise, it did become a very significant day for the air war.

The day began ominously quiet and remained so until late in the afternoon, then formations of aircraft began to be detected over the Channel. R.A.F. squadrons sent up to intercept, reported enemy aircraft as far as the eye could see. It was the largest concentration of enemy aircraft yet seen, but instead of making for Fighter Command's airfields, the aerial armada turned towards London. The change in the Luftwaffe's tactics was to have a profound effect. For the population of London the agony of prolonged and sustained bombing had begun, but for the R.A.F's. fighter squadrons there was a vital respite in the pounding of their airfields.

In the local area the siren eventually sounded at 5.25 p.m. and just over an hour later bombs fell in the sea off the Grand Hotel at Frinton.

Frinton, 7th September 1940. Men of the 6th Battalion Royal Scots Fusiliers in The Esplanade, opposite The Crescent. Disguised pillboxes line the cliff top. *I. W. M. H3979*

IMPORTANT NOTICE

To the inhabitants of certain towns in Defence Areas who have received instructions to be ready to leave the towns at short notice.

This leaflet is being distributed throughout the country. You will want to know how it affects you, in view of the instructions you have received to be ready to leave the town at short notice.
When evacuation from the town is ordered you will receive definite instructions from the Police. If, for any reason, you receive no order for evacuation from the Police, or if the order is cancelled, you must obey the instructions contained in this leaflet and STAY WHERE YOU ARE.

Issued by the Ministry of Information on behalf of the War Office and the Ministry of Home Security

STAY WHERE YOU ARE

IF this island is invaded by sea or air everyone who is not under orders must stay where he or she is. This is not simply advice: it is an order from the Government, and you must obey it just as soldiers obey their orders. Your order is "Stay Put," **but remember that this does not apply until invasion comes.**

WHY MUST I STAY PUT?

Because in France, Holland and Belgium, the Germans were helped by the people who took flight before them. Great crowds of refugees blocked all roads. The soldiers who could have defended them could not get at the enemy. The enemy used the refugees as a human shield. These refugees were got out on to the roads by rumour and false orders. Do not be caught out in this way. Do not take any notice of any story telling what the enemy has done or where he is. Do not take orders except from the Military, the Police, the Home Guard (L.D.V.) and the A.R.P. authorities or wardens.

WHAT WILL HAPPEN TO ME IF I DON'T STAY PUT?

If you do not stay put you will stand a very good chance of being killed. The enemy may machine-gun you from the air in order to increase panic, or you may run into enemy forces which have landed behind you. An official German message was captured in Belgium which ran :

> "Watch for civilian refugees on the roads. Harass them as much as possible."

Our soldiers will be hurrying to drive back the invader and will not be able to stop and help you. On the contrary, they will have to turn *you* off the roads so that they can get at the enemy. You will not have reached safety and you will have done just what the enemy wanted you to do.

HOW SHALL I PREPARE TO STAY PUT?

Make ready your air-raid shelter; if you have no shelter, prepare one. Advice can be obtained from your local Air Raid Warden or in "Your Home as an Air-raid Shelter," the Government booklet which tells you how to prepare a shelter in your house that will be strong enough to protect you against stray shots and falling metal. If you can have a trench ready in your garden or field, so much the better, especially if you live where there is likely to be danger from shell-fire.

HOW CAN I HELP?

You can help by setting a good example to others. Civilians who try to join in the fight are more likely to get in the way than to help. The defeat of an enemy attack is the task of the armed forces which include the Home Guard, so if you wish to fight enrol in the Home Guard. If there is no vacancy for you at the moment, register your name for enrolment and you will be called upon as soon as the Army is ready to employ you. For those who cannot join, there are many ways in which the Military and Home Guard may need your help in their preparations. Find out what you can do to help in any local defence work that is going on, and be ready to turn your hand to anything if asked by the Military or Home Guard to do so.

If you are responsible for the safety of a factory or some other important building, get in touch with the nearest military authority. You will then be told how your defence should fit in with the military organisation and plans.

WHAT SHALL I DO IF THE INVADER COMES MY WAY?

If fighting by organised forces is going on in your district and you have no special duties elsewhere, go to your shelter and stay there till the battle is past. Do not attempt to join in the fight. Behave as if an air-raid were going on. The enemy will seldom turn aside to attack separate houses.

But if small parties are going about threatening persons and property in an area not under enemy control and come your way, you have the right of every man and woman to do what you can to protect yourself, your family and your home.

STAY PUT.

It's easy to say. When the time comes it may be hard to do. But you have got to do it; and in doing it you will be fighting Britain's battle as bravely as a soldier.

(382)22478 Wt 23640—P 630 204,000 8/40 E & S (Printed in England)

Monday, 9 September

Bomber Command was making every effort to disrupt the assembly of an invasion fleet on the other side of the Channel. As part of that process, at 5.45 in the morning eight Wellingtons from 149 Squadron took off from their base at R.A.F. Mildenhall in Suffolk, to bomb enemy shipping, barges and harbour installations at Neuer, Binnenhaven and Boulogne. Two aircraft failed to return to base and were logged as missing. Wellington P9245, was believed to have been hit by lightening and crashed into the sea. Pilot Officer Parish, the pilot, swam ashore between Frinton and Holland–on–Sea, but it is believed the remainder of the crew perished.

Wellington MkIc, P9245, coded OJ–W

S/Ldr Andrews	Captain
P/O Parish	Pilot
Sgt Payne	Observer
Sgt Brane	W/T Operator
Sgt Bull	Air Gunner
P/O Searles	Air Gunner

Monday, 16 September

At 3.30 a.m. two incendiary bombs were reported at Great Holland.

Tuesday, 17 September

Just after 3 a.m., coastal searchlights picked out a barrage balloon floating on the sea 2 miles off Frinton.

Wednesday, 18 September

In the late evening an unexploded cannon shell was found.

Saturday, 21 September

The first damage to property in the District was caused in the afternoon. At just after 3 p.m. and without warning from the siren, a lone aircraft dropped four high–explosive bombs north of the railway line at Frinton and another four near the pier at Walton. Damage was caused to Mr Baker's house, next to Baker's Garage in Pole Barn Lane and at Walton, windows were broken along the full length of the seafront from Southcliff almost to the Albion Hotel.

Wednesday, 25 September

The air raid siren had been sounded at 8.40 p.m. and at 11.05 p.m. a parachute mine landed by the Little Clacton Road at Great Holland and badly damaged the house *Clan Gordon*. After no further incidents in the District the 'all clear' sounded at 1.20 in the morning.

6th Battalion Royal Scots Fusiliers at the Naze golf course, September 1940.
Above. The view is towards the Tamarisk seawall (destroyed in the 1953 floods) and Harwich. The pillbox, camouflaged to represent a hut, is still in place today. *I. W. M. H4045*
Below. From the same location, looking out to sea, anti-aircraft practice at balloons using tripod mounted Bren light machine-guns. *I. W. M. H4048*

Thursday, 26 September

At 12.50 p.m. an incendiary bomb was reported at Great Holland.

Sunday, 29 September

At 10.55 a.m. the air raid siren sounded just as 17 high–explosive bombs fell near the Pier and the Bath House Meadow at Walton. No significant damage was believed to have been caused.

Monday, 30 September

An air raid warning was in force for the last four hours of the evening and at 10.05 p.m. one incendiary and two high–explosive bombs were reported at Kirby. An hour and a quarter later the A.R.P. logged a crashed aircraft, but no amplifying details.

Thursday, 3 October

A number of individual enemy aircraft were plotted in and around the District during the late morning. Just after 1.30 p.m. soldiers at the Naze searchlight site opened fire at a low flying Dornier aircraft. The only anti–aircraft armament available at that time were tripod mounted light machine-guns.

For the first few years of the war the only anti-aircraft defences in the Frinton & Walton District were tripod mounted light machine-guns. Here the use of a Bren gun is staged for the cameramen. *I. W. M. H2349*

Just after 4 p.m. a couple of high–explosive bombs fell some distance from the Frinton golf course searchlight site, but no damage was reported.

Saturday, 5 October

During the night there was little aerial activity, probably due to the bad weather and dense cloud cover, but at 2.40 a.m. an air raid alert commenced and 15 minutes later incendiary and high–explosive bombs fell between Frinton and Great Holland. Approximately 50 incendiary bombs fell, mostly in Great Holland and in the vicinity of the Frinton Tennis Club, together with two 'oil' bombs at Great Holland; none of which were reported to have caused any material damage. One high explosive bomb at Meer's Farm, Frinton resulted in many broken windows and some minor damage to properties in Witton Wood Road and in Frinton Road between Turpin's Lane and Village Way.

Sunday, 6 October

At 13.30 p.m. a Dornier aircraft attacked the Shipwash Light–vessel with machine–gun fire.

At 6.40 p.m. the Holland Coastguard look–out post reported to the Walton Coastguards that a vessel was drifting just offshore in the direction of Walton. The vessel was showing lights and appeared to be in distress. Half an hour later the lifeboat was launched to assist what was believed to be the *Scotch Thistle.* The lifeboat searched all night but found no sign of the vessel and returned to her station at 9 a.m. the next morning. The Clacton lifeboat also searched and later reported that it was believed the vessel, a drifter, had hit the beach at Frinton, but was not there when day broke.

Thursday, 10 October

Without a siren warning, at 3.25 a.m. four high–explosive bombs fell at Kirby Cross. Slight damage was caused to eight properties, most on the northern side of Frinton Road opposite the Coronation Garage. One bomb was unexploded.

Friday, 11 October

At 10.10 p.m., three high–explosive bombs fell at Horsey Island.

Saturday, 12 October

At about 8.00 p.m. the Felixstowe Observer Corps post monitored a German aircraft, thought to be a Junkers Ju88, closing the coast from the south–east, then turning towards the south–west and diving into the sea. The aircraft was seen to fall on the Naze side of the Harwich deep water channel, just off Dovercourt. The following day a landing wheel and two cylinders were washed up near Landguard Fort which confirmed the German origin, but there was no sign of the crew.

Tuesday, 15 October

The 50th (Holding) Battalion was one of the units created in 1940 to swell the Army's ranks. It was established in Suffolk and in early October 1940, whilst at Great Glemham in East Suffolk, the unit was redesignated as the 8th Battalion of the Suffolk Regiment. The Commanding Officer noted that the men were young and keen, but inexperienced and had received very little training.

On 15th October the new battalion arrived in Frinton and Walton to relieve 6th Battalion Royal Scots Fusiliers in the duties of coastal defence. 'A' Company went to the Naze, 'C' Company covered the town of Walton, 'B' Company took the ground between Walton Railway Station and Pole Barn Lane and 'D' Company covered the town of Frinton. The HQ Company occupied the hinterland centred along the length of Elm Tree Avenue, Ashes Corner and the Kirby Road as far as Cole's Lane.

Just before 7.30 that evening, 'D' Company's area received the welcome of three high–explosive bombs which landed in the vicinity of the Naze Tower.

Wednesday, 16 October

At 5.25 p.m., a further three high–explosive bombs fell on the Naze golf course.

Just before 10.30 p.m., the Coastguards reported an aircraft down in the sea close to the Barrow Deep and some 9 miles offshore from Holland Haven.

Thursday, 17 October

At 7.30 a.m. a mine was washed ashore.

Saturday, 19 October

At 8.20 p.m. while an air raid warning was in force, six high–explosive bombs fell on Walton marshes and at Kirby. Just before 11.00 p.m. another high–explosive bomb fell at Sandy Hook. No damage to property was reported from either incident.

Sunday, 20 October

The 'all clear' from the previous evening's air raid warning sounded just before 2.30 a.m. At 7 a.m. five high–explosive bombs fell at Frinton and 25 minutes later another six fell at Great Holland.

No damage was reported in Great Holland, but in Frinton the bombs fell in the residential area to the east of the town between Pole Barn Lane and The Esplanade. The line of bombs ran east–west leaving a series of craters: in the back garden of *Sheldon* in Hadleigh Road; *Gaythorne's* garden at the corner of Hadleigh Road and Eton Road; the back gardens of *Manderville* and *Cumnor* in Eton Road; in front of *Sweet Briar's* garage in Winchester Road and in the front garden of *Hollywood* at the corner of Winchester Road and The Esplanade. None of the houses were hit and damage was slight.

During an alert that evening one further high–explosive bomb fell in the vicinity of *The Grand Hotel* at Frinton, but no damage was reported.

Tuesday, 22 October

The air raid warning sounded at 2.40 a.m. and 20 minutes later one high–explosive and two 'oil' bombs fell at Kirby. No damage was reported.

Sunday, 27 October

When the air raid warning sounded for the second time that day, just after 4.30 p.m., soldiers at the Naze watched as R.A.F. fighters engaged a large number of enemy aircraft.

Monday, 28 October

The air raid warning sounded at 2.45 in the afternoon and just five minutes later a lone Dornier bomber appeared over Walton and dropped 20 high–explosive bombs in a line between the Pier and New House Farm in Kirby Road. Light machine–gun fire was directed at the aircraft, but with no apparent results. Some of the bombs fell in the sea but the remainder destroyed or seriously damaged eight houses.

Local lifeboatman Ted Oxley watched as the bombs fell, 'in pairs and like two strings of sausages'. The bowling green, on the cliff edge just above the Pier Hotel was hit; it was being used for storing beach huts and a shower of timber was blown into the air. The companion bomb fell in Agar Road Approach, behind the tall houses of the Crescent, fracturing the sewer pipe and raising a cloud of red dust. At the corner of the carpark the Council's blacksmith's shop was severely damaged.

The next bomb partly demolished Doctor Wheatley's home, *Strathmore [Stratheden]*, on the corner of Station Street and Church Road and severely damaged the carpark office on the other side of Station Street. Half way down Church Road, numbers 29 and 31 were destroyed and number 27 was partly demolished. Two craters were left in the cemetery [now the memorial gardens], the Mortuary was damaged, a boundary wall was partly demolished and tomb stones were displaced.

In Walton Road the semi–detached bungalow *Narvic* was destroyed and next door *Westway* and *Crossways* were badly damaged. A crater lay in the front garden of *Crossways.*

In Kirby Road, opposite what later became the entrance to the Martello Caravan Camp, a slaughter house shed was badly damaged and the main sewer pipe under the road was fractured. The line of bombs continued on to New House Farm where some minor damage was reported.

Lesser damage was caused to properties in a wide swathe either side of the bomb line. Eighty houses suffered minor damage, but fortunately only two people were hurt.

Tuesday, 29 October

At 8.35 p.m. an aircraft was seen to crash into the sea half a mile offshore at Holland Haven. The Clacton lifeboat was launched as a man was reported to be in the water, but nothing was found. The following afternoon parts of a German aircraft were washed up on the shore at Clacton.

Thursday, 31 October

At about 8 p.m. three incendiary bombs were reported at Great Holland.

Friday, 1 November

223 Infantry Brigade was formed, with an H.Q. established at Colchester. The brigade temporarily came under the command structure of the resident 15th (Scottish) Division, but it was later to become part of the new 'Essex Division', which was in the process of forming to take over responsibility for defence of the Essex coastline. 223 Infantry Brigade consisted of four infantry battalions and was allocated defence of the beaches between the Rivers Stour and Blackwater:

10th Essex – Harwich.
8th Suffolks – Frinton and Walton.
6th Northants. – Clacton.
10th Yorks & Lancs. – Brightlingsea and Tollesbury.

Saturday, 2 November

The 6th Battalion, Royal Scots Fusiliers handed over operational control of the Walton and Frinton coastal defence sector to the 8th Suffolks. The new battalion had as its objectives:

(a) To resist enemy landings on the coast.
(b) To destroy enemy landed from aircraft or by parachute in the battalion's sector.
(c) To resist enemy attack from landward side.
(d) To prevent sabotage, by enemy agents already in the country, on certain 'Vulnerable Points'.
(e) Any combination of the above.

As with previous units' orders, the battalion's defence plan added, "There will be NO WITHDRAWAL. Sections will fight to LAST MAN and LAST ROUND in positions assigned to them irrespective of what may happen to sections on their flanks and rear."

Thursday, 7 November

In the late afternoon an aircraft was reported down in the sea 2½ miles south–east of Frinton. Just after 5 p.m. the naval authorities at Harwich requested the lifeboat to conduct a search. The lifeboat was out until 9.15 in the evening but reported nothing seen in the area except some patches of oil.

Further offshore the trawler *William Wesney* was mined and sank one mile off South Ship Head. In the Wallet, off Holland–on–Sea, the Clacton lifeboat went to the assistance of H.M. Drifter *Reed* which had been mined. Only one survivor was found. He was taken ashore, but died later in hospital.

The Naze golf course, February 1941.

Lines of barbed wire and recently dug ditches cross the fairways (see photo page 35). Whether the latter were constructed as a result of F/O Howell's impromptu landing on 30th May, remains speculation.

The RDF (radar) site lies on the cliff edge between the Naze Tower and Tower breakwater. The shadows of the 'transmit' and 'receive' aerials can be seen at either end of a short zig-zag defensive trench. Later, in May 1942, the two aerials were combined into a single aerial erected on top of the Naze Tower.

R.A.F. photograph

Wednesday, 13 November

Without warning just before 3 a.m., one 'oil' bomb and two high–explosive bombs fell at the Naze on Harper's Tennis Courts and in the vicinity of the Foundry. There were no casualties and damage to houses was of a relatively minor nature, mainly broken windows and cracked plasterwork, but the area of damage was extensive: covering the full length of Hall Lane and parts of the roads leading from it, part of Naze Park Road and First Avenue, and East Terrace including the *Eastcliff Hotel.* A crater from the oil bomb marked its point of impact at the tennis courts on the opposite side of Hall Lane to the hotel.

At 6 a.m. four high–explosive bombs fell on Horsey Island and just a few minutes afterwards the siren sounded, but there were no further bombs and the 'all clear' followed an hour later.

In the evening just after 7.30, while another air raid warning was in force, the Kirby searchlight unit reported two high–explosive bombs between Kirby and Frinton, but no damage.

Saturday, 16 November

At 2 p.m. a Dornier aircraft attacked the East Swin Light–vessel and holed it in a few places.

Monday, 18 November

During mid–afternoon, soldiers at the Naze reported a convoy being attacked some 10 miles offshore from Frinton.

Just before 8.30 in the evening, men from the Naze searchlight sites, at the Jubilee Ground and golf course, engaged a low flying aircraft with machine–gun fire.

Tuesday, 19 November

Just after 10 a.m. the North East Swin Light–vessel intercepted a 'Mayday' signal from the *S.S. Solda* and relayed the message to Walton Coastguards. The R.N.L.I. report continues:

"At 10.10 a.m. a message was received from the coastguard that a vessel near the N.E.Swin Light–vessel had been attacked by German aeroplanes. A light south–west breeze was blowing, with a moderate sea. At 11 a.m. the motor lifeboat *E.M.E.D.* was launched and went to the North East Gunfleet. Here she spoke to a patrol boat, which had six wounded and one dead man on board, all belonging to a steamer which had been bombed and machine–gunned. Continuing on her way, the lifeboat found the steamer, the *Folda,* of Leith, for which she was in search. The steamer's steering gear and engines had been damaged, and the master asked the lifeboat to stand by until the arrival of a tug. The tug took her in tow and the lifeboat escorted them to the entrance of Harwich Harbour..."

Just before five in the afternoon, the Coastguards learned that a Hurricane aircraft had crashed, but the position was unknown. The lifeboat had just completed her escort duty to Harwich and while there was given the message of the aircraft reported to have crashed somewhere near the Naze. The lifeboat returned to Walton and closed the shore by the Coastguard Station to seek further information. The Coxswain was instructed to conduct a search on passage back to the lifeboat's moorings in the Backwaters.

Having found no sign of the aircraft the lifeboat reached its moorings at 7.30 in the evening just as the air raid siren sounded. Forty five minutes later three bombs fell at Kirby and Walton, but no damage was reported.

Thursday, 21 November

At 11.55 a.m. the 'all clear' was sounded after the second air raid warning of the day. Half an hour later a Dornier Do215 bomber flew over Walton and was engaged by light machine–gun fire from men of the 8th Suffolks and the searchlight detachment at the Jubilee Ground, as it dropped nine high–explosive bombs by Walton School in Standley Road; one did not explode. The line of bombs ran from the boating lake, across the bottom of Saville Street and behind the school, parallel with Standley Road.

Two houses were destroyed in Saville Street (numbers 71 and 73) near the junction with Standley Road. Next door, Saville Hall was severely damaged, so much so that later it had to be demolished. It was an old building and used as a furniture store by Snare's of the High Street. The school had windows broken, shrapnel holes in the walls and tiles dislodged and broken. Other minor damage was confined mainly to the remaining houses in the terrace at the end of Saville Street.

Two seriously injured casualties were reported; one being Dr McMillan who had been in his car which was wrecked.

Sunday, 24 November

During an early evening air raid alert, one high–explosive bomb fell in a field at Walton near New House Farm and close to the 8th Suffolk's Battalion H.Q. in Kirby Road. Apart from broken glass at the farm there was no other damage.

Wednesday, 27 November

During an early morning air raid alert, a number of incendiary bombs were dropped on Frinton golf course; the number reported varying between seven and twenty. No damage was caused.

After a reappraisal of night time anti–aircraft defences a restructuring of the searchlight locations was brought into effect. Instead of an even spread of single lights throughout the area, units were grouped into clusters of three, so that one light could act as a master beam and the other two could follow in parallel. To achieve this the Beaumont and Lower Kirby lights were moved to the Naze site and the Hodgnoll's Farm site at Great Holland moved to make a cluster in Clacton. The remaining four sites in the district, which were all on the coast (the Naze Jubilee Ground, Walton Burnt House Farm, Frinton golf club and Holland Haven), became single beam coastal sites and operated as satellites of one of the clusters.

Thursday, 28 November

Just after midnight, 2/Lt Leslie Stewart M.C. of the 8th Suffolks was involved in a motor cycle accident while visiting the battalion's 'D' Company positions in Frinton as Duty Officer. He subsequently died of his injuries. He had been awarded the Military Cross earlier in the year during the fighting in France. At that time he had found himself as part of the 'Syme' Battalion in the 'Beauman' Division – *ad hoc* units named after their commanding officers and formed 'in the field' from smaller units neither intended nor trained for deployment as front line infantry. The award was made for successfully mining and closing a main road block while under mortar and machine gun fire. He was 22 years old.

Friday, 29 November

At 6.35 p.m., ten minutes after the air raid siren had sounded, seven high–explosive bombs fell at Great Holland, but no damage was caused.

Wednesday, 4 December

Just after 7.30 p.m. the single beam searchlight detachment at the Naze Jubilee Ground fired their light anti–aircraft machine–gun at a Heinkel He111 which had been illuminated by the cluster site at the Naze golf course. No resulting effect was reported.

Tuesday, 10 December

At five minutes past four in the afternoon, a bomber, recognised as a Dornier Do215 by soldiers from the 8th Suffolks, flew over Walton and dropped two bombs on the town [probably mines].

There was no siren warning but the aircraft's approach from the north had been observed by those on the ground whose attention had been drawn by the sound of anti–aircraft gunfire in the Harwich direction.

One bomb landed in the boating lake and it is believed did not explode, while the other landed amongst a block of tall terraced houses on the Parade, just behind the Pier Hotel. The houses were being used as billets for some of the 8th Suffolk's 'C' Company. Fortunately the houses were empty at the time, except for one soldier who had been taking a bath and when the dust settled found himself exposed to the elements. He had a lucky escape

Three houses in the terrace were totally destroyed, leaving a crater 20 feet across and 8 feet deep, and the remaining houses were so badly damaged that they had to be pulled down. Two houses on the other side of the road, numbers 1 and 2 New Pier Street, also had to be demolished as they were so badly damaged.

Damage to other property in the surrounding streets was widespread, but most was of a minor nature. Only two people required hospital treatment and both were thought not to be serious.

Friday, 13 December

At 7.15 p.m. two unexploded parachute mines were found near the Frinton Water Tower. They were subsequently immobilised.

Sunday, 15 December

At 2.20 p.m. two unexploded parachute mines were found at Great Holland.

Monday, 16 December

At midday the Shipwash Light–vessel was attacked by machine–gun fire from an aircraft, wounding one man.

Saturday, 21 December

In the late afternoon the searchlight detachment at the Naze Jubilee Ground reported a mine in the sea off the Naze.

Monday, 23 December

A collapsible rubber boat from a German aircraft was washed ashore at Frinton. It was empty except for its inflating apparatus. A German airman's helmet was found nearby.

Wednesday, 25 December

In the morning a soldier from the 8th Suffolks was killed when a 'cutter mine' exploded as he was loading it onto a lorry in Queen's Road Frinton. Warnings about moving such items had been issued. Only two days previously two of these devices, called 'cutter mines', had been washed ashore at Clacton. Cone shaped, with a rounded base, they were quite small at only 2½ feet long and just over 1 foot wide at the base. They were believed to be used for destroying minefields.

Tuesday, 31 December

At 2 p.m. a Junkers Ju88 bomber was fired on with light machine–guns by the searchlight detachments at the Naze golf course and at Holland Haven. The aircraft continued on towards Clacton where it received a similar reception from another searchlight post before continuing west with smoke reported to be coming from its tail.

Whilst over Frinton, the Ju88 dropped a single high–explosive bomb which fell between Queen's Road and The Crescent, behind the building being used as a cookhouse by the 8th Suffolks 'D' Company. Damage was caused to the surrounding houses and four soldiers were cut by flying glass.

Walton-on-the-Naze, February 1941.

Some of the results of the 1940 bombing can be seen. A line of craters (top) lie behind the school and the Bath House meadow. The devastation caused to the block of houses on The Parade by the Pier Hotel on 10th Dec. is very evident. Likewise, at the very bottom of the picture, the rubble that was *Strathmore* (28th Oct) lies at the junction of Church Road and Station Street. One of the gaps made in the Pier can be seen and the barge *Martha* lies beached at the end of Standley Road.

R.A.F. photograph

1941

Sunday, 19 January

Just after 1 a.m. the Coastguard watchman at Walton saw a flare 1½ miles to the south–east; the sailing barge *Martha* was being driven ashore. The lifeboat was called out, while a team from the Coastguard Station made their way along the sea front with line throwing gear. Arriving at the scene, the Coastguards fired a line by rocket from the shore, but the strong onshore wind prevented it reaching the barge. It was then up to the lifeboat. The R.N.L.I. report of the incident continues:

"In the early morning, flares were seen burning about half a mile north of the pier at Walton, close to the beach. A south–easterly gale was blowing, with squalls of rain and snow; the night was very dark; a heavy sea was running dead on shore. The motor lifeboat *E.M.E.D.* put off from her moorings at the end of the pier at five minutes past two, and in a quarter of an hour she found the barge *Martha,* of Rochester. The barge had anchored, but her anchor had not held, and she had gone ashore stern first. There she lay in six feet of water, with the seas breaking right over her. Her crew of three men could be seen in the fore rigging. Handling the lifeboat very skilfully the coxswain brought her alongside the barge, and in spite of the high seas held her there long enough for the three men to jump aboard her from the barge's rigging. Then he brought her safely out of the breakers, undamaged, although in the shallow water her keel had struck the bottom three times. She was back at her station again just before three in the morning.

It was a skilful and courageous rescue, and the Institution made the following awards:

To Coxswain Thomas H.Bloom, the bronze medal for gallantry, with a copy of the vote inscribed on vellum;

To Thomas Claude Brooke, the motor–mechanic, the bronze medal for gallantry, with a copy of the vote inscribed on vellum;

To the coxswain and each member of the crew a special reward of £2, in addition to the reward on the ordinary scale."

The day did not end there for the lifeboatmen. Twelve hours later, in mid afternoon, the Sunk Light–vessel signalled that a vessel half a mile from her had been bombed by aircraft. The *S.S. Bonnington Court,* outbound from Harwich, had been hit amidships and was on fire aft. The lifeboat was launched to assist, but later was recalled when it was learned that naval craft had taken off the survivors before the ship sank. The lifeboat returned to her moorings at 9 p.m.

At 7.35 p.m., one high–explosive bomb fell in the sea off the Naze.

Monday, 20 January

At 1.35 p.m. there was a suspected unexploded bomb at *Hillcrest,* Walton.

Tuesday, 21 January

Just before 11 a.m. the Coastguards reported that the Sunk Light–vessel was being bombed, one bomb landing just 10 feet from the vessel. An hour later an aircraft machine–gunned parts of Frinton and Walton.

Wednesday, 22 January

At about 9.30 a.m., a mine exploded at sea off Walton, causing minor damage to the chimney stacks of a few houses at The Parade (near the Railway Station) and at Southcliff.

Thursday, 23 January

The Sunk Light–vessel sank; probably as a result of the bombing two days previously. All the crew were brought ashore by a trawler.

Sunday, 26 January – Saturday, 1 February

During the evening of January 26th, the *S.S. Belgia*, of Gothenburg, was bombed by German aircraft and set on fire. Her crew abandoned ship and after drifting down the Wallet during the night, she eventually went aground on Frinton beach, opposite the Queen's Hotel, just before four in the morning.

By daybreak The Admiralty Salvage Officer from Harwich and the Walton Coastguard Station Officer were at the scene. The Salvage Officer sought the help of the lifeboat in attempting to refloat the steamer, and at 11.15 a.m. the *E.M.E.D.* set off with fire pumps, firemen and a salvage party. The pumps were put in the boarding boat which was towed by the lifeboat. Work on the vessel continued until darkness fell.

The next day the weather was too rough for any salvage work to be done, but the lifeboat was called upon again on January 29th and 30th. On February 1st the lifeboat was out for most of the day, while two tugs attempted to refloat the steamer, but the effort was unsuccessful.

Friday, 7 February

During a tour of the Eastern Counties, the Prime Minister, The Rt. Hon. Winston Churchill, took time out at Colchester to call on the unit he had commanded during the First World War – the 6th Battalion, Royal Scots Fusiliers.

Then it was on to the coast to view the defence works being prepared by the 8th Suffolks at Frinton and Walton. During the visit, the Battalion's 'B' Company marched past the Prime Minister, along Central Avenue in Frinton Park Estate.

An hour after the official party departed and just half a mile along the cliffs from the march past, some defence land mines exploded, breaking glass in the windows of houses on The Esplanade at Frinton. Wetter weather during the winter often resulted in movement of the cliffs and such self detonations were to become a frequent hazard.

7th February 1941. Men from 'B' Company of the Suffolk Regiment's 8th Battalion march past Winston Churchill along Central Avenue in Frinton Park Estate. A road block lies on the bridge over the railway line (far left). *I. W. M. H7064*

Tuesday, 11 February

At 1.15 a.m. some more defence land mines exploded, but no damage was reported.

Wednesday, 12 February

About an hour before midnight there were further explosions from defence land mines along the Frinton seafront, causing numerous broken windows, mainly to properties on The Esplanade between Connaught Avenue and Queen's Road.

Thursday, 13 February

At 5.30 a.m., defence land mines exploded on the cliffs by Frinton Park Estate. Glass was broken in a few houses at The Leas, at the end of Central Avenue.

Just before 9 p.m., during an air raid alert, eight unexploded bombs were reported at Frinton.

Friday, 14 February

Defence land mines exploded at 7.45 a.m., along the Walton seafront this time, on the cliffs opposite Station Gardens, causing broken windows and minor damage to surrounding houses at Southcliff, one end of Woodberry Way, The Parade and LNER property at the Railway Station.

Frinton-on-Sea, 10th February 1941.

Pill boxes and barbed wire line the cliff top. The seaward end of Connaught Avenue, by the Gun Garden, is sealed by concrete blocks. On the cliff top opposite the Grand Hotel (at the bottom of the picture) lies the twin 6-inch gun battery. The *S.S. Belgia* lies aground just offshore.

R.A.F. photograph

As conditions at sea were favourable, the help of the lifeboat was again requested for another attempt to refloat the *S.S. Belgia* off Frinton beach. The lifeboat left at 11.35 in the morning and stood by until 1.30 when the steamer was successfully refloated. The *Belgia* was towed to Harwich, but on route the lifeboat took off the salvage party and landed them at Walton Pier later in the afternoon.

Saturday, 15 February

At 8.15 p.m. the Observer Corps reported an enormous flash in the sky, following anti–aircraft fire in the area just offshore between the Naze and Felixstowe.

Tuesday, 18 February

This was an active day for enemy raiders over the District. The air raid siren sounded three times during the day and in total the alert was in force for 9¾ hours.

The first alert was at 2.35 a.m. An hour later two high–explosive bombs fell at Great Holland and one high–explosive and three 'oil' bombs at Ashes Farm, Walton. There was no damage to property at either place. An hour later two high–explosive bombs and one unexploded bomb fell on the foreshore at Frinton, also without causing damage. The 'all clear' finally sounded just after 7 a.m.

The respite was a short 2½ hours before the second warning sounded, which lasted until just before midday, this time without incident. Half an hour after the 'all clear', two parachute mines fell in the vicinity of Stone Point at the Naze: one did not explode.

During the third alert, which began in the afternoon at 2.35., the naval authorities asked for the services of the lifeboat to destroy a mine floating 150 yards off Walton Pier. The lifeboat was launched an hour later, with the additional crew of the Walton Coastguard Station Officer and a naval rating with a gun. The mine was found and sunk, but while the lifeboat was out, explosions of a different kind occurred not too far away, as an aircraft dropped 12 high–explosive bombs in the sea off Walton at 4.30 p.m. At the same time, Prince's Esplanade at Walton was machine–gunned.

For the last time that day the 'all clear' sounded at 5.20 p.m.

Wednesday, 26 February

Just after midnight the local A.R.P. organisation received a warning of enemy airmen at large. There were no further reports concerning this incident or its outcome.

Tuesday, 4 March

The air raid warning sounded at 7.30 p.m. and just ten minutes later seven high–explosive bombs (a mixture of 50kg bombs and at least one 250kg bomb) fell at Walton, on land between the Boating Lake and Foundry Creek, that was later to become the Eastcliff Caravan Park.

Friday, 7 March

At 4 p.m. an unexploded bomb was reported at Island Lane, Kirby.

A defensive position is manned at the end of Woodberry Way, Walton, during a mock invasion exercise, 11th/12th March 1941. *I. W. M. H7942*

Monday, 17 March

In the morning, two defence land mines exploded on Frinton seafront, one at about 6.40 a.m. and the other at about 9.30 a.m. Minor damage and broken glass occurred along a length of The Esplanade from *The Willows* near Fourth Avenue, past the end of Connaught Avenue, to *The Bungalow* near Queen's Road. For many of these seafront properties it was the second time of such damage and for some it was not to be the last. A few properties in Fourth Avenue, the lower part of Connaught Avenue and Harold Road also suffered the effects this time.

Tuesday, 18 March

Another defence land mine exploded at 7.30 a.m. on Frinton seafront, approximately opposite the Grand Hotel, adding to the broken glass in the vicinity.

Saturday, 22 March

There were four air raid 'red alert' periods during the afternoon. The final alert began at 4.45 and half an hour later two parachute mines fell just outside the District to the west of Lower Kirby, by the junction of Sneating Hall Lane and Dale Hill. Only one mine exploded and the other was later rendered safe by the Harwich naval authorities. There was minimal damage reported inside the District.

Wednesday, 26 March

In Frinton at 9.30 p.m., defence land mines again self detonated on the cliff edge; eight exploded half way between Connaught Avenue and Queen's Road and three others at the end of Connaught Avenue. This time the houses opposite appear to have escaped further damage.

Wednesday, 2 April

Just after 4 p.m., further cliff movement at Frinton caused more mines to explode. This time it was estimated that twenty mines self detonated opposite the house *Apple Trees,* eight of them on the cliff face and twelve on the Greensward at the cliff top. Every house on The Esplanade between Connaught Avenue and Queen's Road reported some form of minor damage. Behind them in Harold Road, three other properties suffered similar damage.

Monday, 7 April

The third air raid warning of the day began at 8.40 p.m. Three hours later two high–explosive bombs (estimated by the military to be 500kg bombs) exploded at Frinton in the garden of *The Retreat,* between Third and Fourth Avenues, half way between The Esplanade and Holland Road. Speculation at the time was that the bombs may have been aimed at the searchlight site a few hundred yards away, which was in operation at the time.

Two houses were so badly damaged that they had to be demolished: *The Retreat,* lying mid–way between Third and Fourth Avenues and *The Croft,* next to it in Third Avenue. The surrounding properties in that part of the Avenues, suffered varying degrees of minor damage, but there were no casualties. Both *The Retreat* and *The Croft* were unoccupied at the time.

Wednesday, 9 April

An air raid warning had remained in force from the previous evening and at about 4 a.m. a Heinkel He111 dropped a single 500Kg high–explosive bomb at the Naze, just to the north east of the Naze Tower. Again it was thought that the bomb had been aimed at the searchlight site only yards away.

Friday, 11 April

Just before midnight of the previous evening, the air raid warning had been sounded and it remained in force for most of the night. At 2 a.m. two high–explosive (believed to be 50kg) bombs fell in a field behind the *High Tree Stores* at the Naze. There were no casualties and no major damage, but minor damage affected the *High*

Tree Stores, Olive Cottages and *Brickfield Cottages* in High Tree Lane. Houses in the immediate vicinity of Naze Park Road, Hall Lane and the length of First Avenue were also affected.

Wednesday, 16 April

At 7 a.m. an aircraft was reported to have been shot down 10 miles east of Clacton, near the north–east end of the Gunfleet sands.

Thursday, 17 April

In the early afternoon, aircraft wreckage was reported in the sea half a mile off Felixstowe. There may have been a connection between this and the incident reported the previous day.

The Duke of Gloucester, the area's Divisional Commander, together with the local Brigade Commander, visited the 8th Suffolks at Frinton and Walton.

Sunday, 20 April

In the early afternoon a dogfight involving R.A.F. fighters and eight Messerschmitt Me110's, took place just off the Naze.

Monday, 21 April

In the early hours of the morning, an aircraft crashed into the sea in flames some 3 miles north–east of the Naze.

The Walton & Frinton lifeboat's motor boarding boat took out the Admiralty Salvage Officer, a diver and equipment, to search offshore of the Queen's Hotel, Frinton, for the *S.S. Belgia's* anchor and cable, which they found and then buoyed. A week later the boarding boat was again used to guide a drifter to the cable and anchor so they could be recovered. Thus, after almost three months, the saga of the *S.S. Belgia* finally came to an end in the local area.

Wednesday, 23 April

At 12.25 in the afternoon the air raid siren sounded. Forty minutes later, six high–explosive bombs fell at Walton and enemy aircraft gunfire broke windows in four houses in Station Street and New Pier Street. There were no casualties and the bombs caused no damage to property. Four of the bombs fell in the sea off Burnt House breakwater, level with the end of the Pier and one (50kg) fell at the Naze, close to what is now the nature reserve, damaging the seawall.

Just before midnight the Walton Coastguards received a message from the Naval Officer In Charge at Brightlingsea that a Hurricane aircraft was down, with a last known position of 3 miles south of Clacton. The Walton and Frinton lifeboat was launched and a search was conducted together with the Clacton lifeboat and a number of craft from Brightlingsea, but nothing was found.

A flight of MkIIC Hurricanes from No. 3 Squadron, 1941. The serial number of the aircraft in the foreground shows it to be very close in the 'production sequence' to the Hurricane flown by Sgt. Richard Brewin on 29th April 1941. *I. W. M. CH3497*

Tuesday, 29 April

In the morning a Hurricane MkIIC, Z3064, from No.3 Squadron, crashed at Stone Point, Walton, killing its 20 year old pilot, Sergeant Richard Brewin.

The story of this incident is related by Group Captain Desmond Scott in his book *'One More Hour'* (Hutchinson 1989). Group Captain Scott, then also a Sergeant pilot with No.3 Squadron and a room mate of 'Dick' Brewin, uses the incident as an example of one of the inexplicable losses the Squadron was experiencing at that time unrelated to enemy action and made all the more puzzling because he considered that, 'if any aircraft was free of vices it was the Hurricane'.

However, the cannon armed Hurricane MkII was still a relatively new variant of the tried and tested Hurricane MkI and had not been in general Squadron service for very long. The major differences were an up–rated Rolls Royce Merlin XX engine and 20 mm cannon armament, but beyond that and the incorporation of numerous minor modifications, there was little difference between the two variants.

Group Captain Scott recounts how the two of them had taken off from R.A.F. Martlesham Heath for an early morning convoy patrol, just as dawn was breaking, Dick Brewin leading. During the course of the patrol they were vectored on to enemy aircraft: 090° at 25,000 feet. Climbing towards and passing through 20,000 feet he watched his companion's aircraft turn on to its back and go rocketing downwards. He followed, but the other aircraft was going down at an incredible speed. He could feel the strain on his own aircraft and knew his friend was in trouble. Thoughts of personal survival took over and with great difficulty he wrenched his own aircraft out of the dive. Returning to Martlesham he learned that an aircraft had been seen to crash at very high speed into the sea off Harwich.

The Squadron's Operations Diary together with the official record of the incident give a different scenario, but the 'peel away' and dive remain the same. The official records relate how Sergeant Brewin was the leader of a section of aircraft during Squadron formation practice flying. When the formation leader gave permission for one section to break away, all the sections went and the whole formation broke up. Radio interference was given as the reason for the confusion, not that it had any real bearing on the loss of Sergeant Brewin's aircraft, which after the break away, dived down at high speed through clouds (which were down to 5,000 feet) and hit the water.

The Observer Corps recorded the crash at 10.53 a.m., in the channel just off Stone Point at the Naze. The lifeboat was launched and two Motor Patrol Boats, Numbers 12 and 29, set off from the Twizzle. The aircraft was found partly submerged with its tail sticking out of the water and the pilot dead in the cockpit. Further action had to wait until the tide fell.

Later the larger remains of the aircraft were salvaged and brought to the Yacht Club. The aircraft was relatively new and there was always the possibility that something could be found to explain the loss. In the end though, it was decided that a technical investigation would not be feasible due to the extent of damage and the cause was finalised as an accident.

Sunday, 4 May

The final alert of the day began in the evening at 10.35. Just over an hour later two high–explosive bombs fell at Frinton Park Estate. The Estate was in the early stages of development just before the war and although the road plan had been laid down, houses were mostly just a patchwork of what was intended, and indeed followed, after the war was over.

Number 66 Marney Way was so badly damaged that it had to be demolished. Fortunately it was unoccupied at the time and unfurnished. Broken windows and minor damage were reported from 13 other properties on the Estate, in Easton Way, Warley Way, The Leas and Audley Way.

Sunday, 11 May

The air raid alert remained in force for most of the night. At 3 a.m. two parachute mines were reported in the Walton area, but no damage. Later at 4.20 a.m., four high–explosive bombs fell at Great Holland. Although there was no serious structural damage, eighteen properties in Kirby Road, Rectory Road and Manor Road suffered minor damage and a further eleven had windows broken .

IMPORTANT NOTICE

This leaflet is being distributed throughout the country. If invasion comes it applies in this town as elsewhere, but before invasion comes those who are not engaged on useful work should leave this town—see special posters and leaflets.

Issued by the Ministry of Information

in co-operation with the War Office and the Ministry of Home Security

Beating the INVADER

A MESSAGE FROM THE PRIME MINISTER

IF invasion comes, everyone—young or old, men and women—will be eager to play their part worthily. By far the greater part of the country will not be immediately involved. Even along our coasts, the greater part will remain unaffected. But where the enemy lands, or tries to land, there will be most violent fighting. Not only will there be the battles when the enemy tries to come ashore, but afterwards there will fall upon his lodgments very heavy British counter-attacks, and all the time the lodgments will be under the heaviest attack by British bombers. The fewer civilians or non-combatants in these areas, the better—apart from essential workers who must remain. So if you are advised by the authorities to leave the place where you live, it is your duty to go elsewhere when you are told to leave When the attack begins, it will be too late to go ; and, unless you receive definite instructions to move, your duty then will be to stay where you are. You will have to get into the safest place you can find, and stay there until the battle is over. For all of you then the order and the duty will be : " STAND FIRM ".

This also applies to people inland if any considerable number of parachutists or air-borne troops are landed in their neighbourhood. Above all, they must not cumber the roads. Like their fellow-countrymen on the coasts, they must " STAND FIRM ". The Home Guard, supported by strong mobile columns wherever the enemy's numbers require it, will immediately come to grips with the invaders, and there is little doubt will soon destroy them.

Throughout the rest of the country where there is no fighting going on and no close cannon fire or rifle fire can be heard, everyone will govern his conduct by the second great order and duty, namely, " CARRY ON ". It may easily be some weeks before the invader has been totally destroyed, that is to say, killed or captured to the last man who has landed on our shores. Meanwhile, all work must be continued to the utmost, and no time lost.

The following notes have been prepared to tell everyone in rather more detail what to do, and they should be carefully studied. Each man and woman should think out a clear plan of personal action in accordance with the general scheme

Winston S. Churchill

STAND FIRM

1. What do I do if fighting breaks out in my neighbourhood?

Keep indoors or in your shelter until the battle is over. If you can have a trench ready in your garden or field, so much the better. You may want to use it for protection if your house is damaged. But if you are at work, or if you have special orders, carry on as long as possible and only take cover when danger approaches. If you are on your way to work, finish your journey if you can.

If you see an enemy tank, or a few enemy soldiers, do not assume that the enemy are in control of the area. What you have seen may be a party sent on in advance, or stragglers from the main body who can easily be rounded up.

This May 1941 leaflet shows that the threat of invasion remained very real at that time, but a month later, events elsewhere dramatically altered the situation.

CARRY ON

2. What do I do in areas which are some way from the fighting?

Stay in your district and carry on. Go to work whether in shop, field, factory or office. Do your shopping, send your children to school until you are told not to. Do not try to go and live somewhere else. Do not use the roads for any unnecessary journey; they must be left free for troop movements even a long way from the district where actual fighting is taking place.

3. Will certain roads and railways be reserved for the use of the Military, even in areas far from the scene of action?

Yes, certain roads will have to be reserved for important troop movements; but such reservations should be only temporary. As far as possible, bus companies and railways will try to maintain essential public services, though it may be necessary to cut these down. Bicyclists and pedestrians may use the roads for journeys to work, unless instructed not to do so.

ADVICE AND ORDERS

4. Whom shall I ask for advice?

The police and A.R.P. wardens.

5. From whom shall I take orders?

In most cases from the police and A.R.P. wardens. But there may be times when you will have to take orders from the military and the Home Guard in uniform.

6. Is there any means by which I can tell that an order is a true order and not faked?

You will generally know your policeman and your A.R.P. wardens by sight, and can trust them. With a bit of common sense you can tell if a soldier is really British or only pretending to be so. If in doubt ask a policeman, or ask a soldier whom you know personally.

INSTRUCTIONS

7. What does it mean when the church bells are rung?

It is a warning to the local garrison that troops have been seen landing from the air in the neighbourhood of the church in question. Church bells will *not* be rung all over the country as a general warning that invasion has taken place. The ringing of church bells in one place will not be taken up in neighbouring churches.

8. Will instructions be given over the wireless?

Yes; so far as possible. But remember that the enemy can overhear any wireless message, so that the wireless cannot be used for instructions which might give him valuable information.

9. In what other ways will instructions be given?

Through the Press; by loudspeaker vans; and perhaps by leaflets and posters. But remember that genuine Government leaflets will be given to you only by the policeman, your A.R.P. warden or your postman; while genuine posters and instructions will be put up only on Ministry of Information notice boards and official sites, such as police stations, post offices, A.R.P. posts, town halls and schools.

FOOD

10. Should I try to lay in extra food?

No. If you have already laid in a stock of food, keep it for a real emergency; but do not add to it. The Government has made arrangements for food supplies.

NEWS

11. Will normal news services continue?

Yes. Careful plans have been made to enable newspapers and wireless broadcasts to carry on, and in case of need there are emergency measures which will bring you the news. But if there should be some temporary breakdown in news supply, it is very important that you should not listen to rumours nor pass them on, but should wait till real news comes through again. Do not use the telephones or send telegrams if you can possibly avoid it.

MOTOR-CARS

12. Should I put my car, lorry or motor-bicycle out of action?

Yes, when you are told to do so by the police, A.R.P. wardens or military; or when it is obvious that there is an immediate risk of its being seized by the enemy—then disable and hide your bicycle and destroy your maps.

13. How should it be put out of action?

Remove distributor head and leads and either empty the tank or remove the carburettor. If you don't know how to do this, find out now from your nearest garage. In the case of diesel engines remove the injection pump and connection. The parts removed must be hidden well away from the vehicle.

THE ENEMY

14. Should I defend myself against the enemy?

The enemy is not likely to turn aside to attack separate houses. If small parties are going about threatening persons and property in an area not under enemy control and come your way, you have the right of every man and woman to do what you can to protect yourself, your family and your home.

GIVE ALL THE HELP YOU CAN TO OUR TROOPS

Do not tell the enemy anything

Do not give him anything

Do not help him in any way

(1649) 59976 Wt. 46381/P1009 250M 5/41 W.P. Ltd. Gp. 8

Monday, 12 May

Again the air raid alert was in force for most of the night. At 1.45 a.m., two high–explosive bombs fell near the Tennis Club at Frinton. There were no casualties and no serious damage to property. Minor damage affected six properties and a further eight had broken windows, mostly on the west side of Second Avenue between Holland Road and the sea.

The 8th Suffolks departed for Colchester Barracks and were relieved for a temporary period by the 1st/6th Lancashire Fusiliers. Ever since the 8th Suffolk's arrival the previous autumn, they had devoted most of their time to the construction of beach defences; the long lines of anti–invasion scaffolding on the beaches bore testament to that. However such work had been to the detriment of their military skills and they now began a four week period of intensive training to rectify the situation.

Monday, 19 May

Again, for much of the night, the air raid alert was in force. At 11.40 p.m. four high–explosive bombs fell at Great Holland, but no damage was reported.

Sunday, 25 May

Just after midday a defence land mine exploded on the Frinton cliffs, at the north end of The Esplanade, opposite *Hollywood*. Damage was limited to broken windows in two houses.

Saturday, 31 May

Between 7 and 8 p.m., five defence land mines exploded on Walton marshes. Four cows were killed and the end house in Saville Street, No.103, was slightly damaged.

Saturday, 7 June

The 8th Suffolks returned to Frinton and Walton from their training period and relieved the 1st/6th Lancashire Fusiliers.

Friday, 20 June

At 12.55 p.m. the naval authorities called on the services of the lifeboat, to assist in the search for an aircraft reported down in the sea 10 miles east of Clacton, in the vicinity of the NE Gunfleet. An hour later the lifeboat was recalled after the naval authorities learned that the aircraft was not down in the sea after all.

Saturday, 21 June

In the early evening, just after 6 p.m., a Hurricane crashed into the sea a mile offshore from Holland–on–Sea. The pilot parachuted to safety and also came down in the sea.

Just over an hour earlier, five Hurricanes from 257 Squadron had left R.A.F. Coltishall, in Norfolk, for a convoy patrol. Leading, was their Commanding Officer, Squadron Leader Robert Stanford Tuck DSO, DFC and Bar: a fighter pilot of considerable reputation, having already notched up over 20 victories. As the patrol came to an uneventful end, Squadron Leader Tuck turned his Hurricane seaward while the other four returned to Coltishall. Alone he headed out across the southern North Sea.

When close to the Dutch coast he was 'bounced' by three Messerschmitt Me109's. In the dogfight that ensued, Squadron Leader Tuck managed to destroy two of the Me109's and damaged the third. His own aircraft, a cannon armed MkIIC Hurricane, Z3152, had been badly damaged and it was an anxious flight back across the North Sea. Finally, when within sight of Clacton, the Hurricane's starboard aileron fell off and with the engine failing, Squadron Leader Tuck was forced to bale out.

He alighted in the sea two miles off the coast and clambered, into his dinghy (a relatively new innovation for fighter pilots, who previously had to rely on a life–jacket only). Rescue was not long in coming; in the form of a sailing barge, but ashore other preparations were being made.

GOOD SHOOTING : Sqn. Ldr. R. R. Stanford-Tuck, D.S.O., D.F.C. and Bar has now been awarded a second Bar to the D.F.C. The miniature swastikas indicate his victories.

An extract from a 1941 magazine. At the time Squadron Leader Robert Stanford Tuck commanded No. 257 Squadron, based at R.A.F. Coltishall in Norfolk and he was one of the R.A.F's. highest scoring fighter pilots. June 21st saw two more victories added to his tally, but he was forced to bale out and was rescued from the sea off Holland-on-Sea. He was no stranger to the North East Essex coast, having spent many holidays at Walton-on-the-Naze when a boy.

News of the incident came in to the Walton Coastguard Station at eight minutes past six, with messages both from the Observer Corps and the Coastguard lookout at Holland Haven. The naval authorities at Brightlingsea despatched rescue boats and ordered both the Walton & Frinton and the Clacton lifeboats to launch and join the search. In addition to the two lifeboats, the motor boarding boat from Walton went as well.

Half an hour after the first report, the Holland lookout post passed a further message to Walton, that the pilot had been picked up by a sailing barge. The news was radioed to the Walton & Frinton lifeboat, *E.M.E.D.*, together with instructions to rendezvous with the barge and investigate. Later, the Clacton Coastguards reported that the military rescue boat *A.R.2,* from Brightlingsea, had been alongside the sailing barge, had taken off Squadron Leader Tuck and was taking him to Brightlingsea, so the *E.M.E.D.* was recalled.

Sunday, 22 June

Germany invaded the U.S.S.R. The news helped explain the lack of enemy aerial activity during recent weeks, as Luftwaffe units had been transferred to the new front.

Monday, 23 June

During an air raid alert in the early hours of the morning, parachute mines were reported. Minor damage and broken windows were reported to four properties in Frinton and Walton.

Except for this rather ill defined incident, June was the first month for a year when no bombs had been dropped in the Frinton & Walton District and the lull was to continue for a further two months. The number and duration of air raid alerts also fell away and the same intensity was not to be experienced in the District for another three years when Hitler's secret weapons began to make their appearance in the skies above southern England.

Tuesday, 24 June

At 3.30 p.m., 25 defence land mines exploded on the shore at Holland Gap, by Frinton golf course. No damage was caused.

Wednesday, 25 June

At 2.20 a.m. the Observer Corps reported that a friendly aircraft had crashed in the sea just off Holland Haven and that a Polish airman had parachuted down near Great Holland Hall.

Just before midnight the previous evening, two Wellingtons of 305 (Polish) Squadron had left R.A.F. Syerston, near Newark in Lincolnshire, for an attack on the docks at Boulogne. One of the Wellingtons, W5723, coded 'F', had an inexperienced crew and Squadron Leader Krelich was flying with them as an additional but experienced pilot.

Over the target there was no cloud, but it was misty and very dark. Squadron Leader Krelich's aircraft made its attack and then turned for home. About 15 miles west of Calais the Wellington was hit by anti–aircraft gunfire from an unidentified ship. The port engine stopped shortly afterwards and the starboard engine soon showed signs of overheating, so the pilot altered course to make for R.A.F. Stradishall, in Suffolk. As the Wellington reached the coast near Clacton, Squadron Leader Krelich ordered the crew to parachute stations.

The rear gunner, Sergeant Frankowski, baled out and came down safely at Great Holland, but the aircraft turned out to sea (speculation would later say, to avoid the damage that a bomber crashing on land could cause) and the remaining crew apparently baled out over the water.

At 2.25 a.m. the Coastguards reported that the bomber was believed to be down in the sea several miles to the east of Clacton and the Clacton lifeboat *J.B.Proudfoot* (on temporary duty at Clacton), was launched at 3.15 a.m. A light south–east wind was blowing and the sea was smooth. Two miles south–east of Holland Haven the lifeboat found the aircraft's Navigator, Pilot Officer Idzikowski, swimming in the water and afterwards picked up the bomber's empty dinghy. As the Navigator was unhurt, the lifeboat continued the search for the other airmen, but without success. After two hours the lifeboat returned to Clacton to land Pilot Officer Idzikowski, then put to sea again and continued the search until 8.30 a.m.

Later in the day, Squadron Leader Krelich's body was found in the sea off Walton, but the other three crew members remained missing: Sergeants Januskiewicz (2nd Pilot), Lewoniec and Witczac (both Wirless Operator/Air Gunners). The wreckage of Wellington W5723 was subsequently salvaged.

Sunday, 29 June

Just before midday a defence land mine exploded at Walton Hall marshes. The cause was thought to have been a wild swan.

Monday, 7 July

H.M. Drifter *Lord St Vincent* was mined and sank 6 miles east of Walton, between West Rocks and the Gunfleet Sands.

Friday, 11 July

At 9.35 in the morning a Hurricane made a wheels up forced landing in a field between Kirby and Thorpe Park. The Hurricane, Z3223, coded 'ER–S', crashed into a hedge and damaged its underside and propeller. The pilot, Squadron Leader Clouston, was only slightly injured. He was a New Zealander and the Commanding Officer of 258 Squadron based at R.A.F. Martlesham Heath.

Just over an hour later a Hawker Hector crashed into the sea 3 miles north–east of the Naze. The biplane was from No.2 Anti–Aircraft Co–operation Unit and had come up from R.A.F. Detling, in Kent, to exercise bombing attacks with M.T.Bs. off Harwich. The two crew were rescued. Pilot Officer Bonner, the pilot, was unhurt but his crewman, Aircraftsman Quinton, was injured and admitted to hospital. The Hawker Hector, K8136, was a write off.

Tuesday, 15 July

An advanced party of 6 officers and 52 other ranks from the 5th Battalion, Duke of Cornwall's Light Infantry arrived in Walton in preparation for a rotation of coastal defence units.

Tuesday, 22 July

The coastal defence infantry battalion changed as part of a wide ranging redeployment of home forces in the Eastern Command area. The 8th Battalion, Suffolk Regiment moved to Theydon Mount, near Epping, in the role of 'counter attack force' in defence of the airfields at R.A.F. North Weald and Stapleford Tawney.

Their place in the Frinton and Walton coastal sector was taken by the 5th Battalion, Duke of Cornwall's Light Infantry (5th D.C.L.I.) which had been on coastal defence duties before, during the latter part of 1940 at Newhaven. The return to such duties was not welcomed and the mood of the moment was recorded by the battalion's diarist, 'After having spent 5 months in G.H.Q. Reserve keen disappointment was felt at the news that the Division was to have a coastal defence role once again.'

5th D.C.L.I. formed one of the four infantry battalions comprising 136 Brigade which was taking over the sector between the Rivers Stour and Colne as part of the overall transfer of responsibility for the Essex coast from the Essex Division to the 45th Division.

Disposition of Army units along the N.E. Essex coast, late July 1941.

5th D.C.L.I.'s area of responsibility was defined by the following boundaries:
To the south – Sandy Point (by the Frinton golf course) to Great Holland, then along the railway line to Weeley.
To the north – the line of Hamford Water, south of Bramble Island to Great Oakley, then to Wix and Horsley Cross.

Individual Company Headquarters were set up in Walton and Frinton as follows:

Battalion HQ – *Merton College*, Kirby Road, Walton. [Since demolished and now the entrance to Elliot's Drive.]
HQ Company – *St Botolphs,* Mill Lane, Walton.
'A' Company – *Ventura,* Prince's Esplanade, Walton.
'B' Company – *Samuel Lewis Home*, Old Hall Lane, the Naze, Walton [since demolished and the site redeveloped].
'C' Company – *Innisfallen,* Woodberry Way, Walton.
'D' Company – *Lintaugh*, Queen's Road, Frinton.

Harvey's Garage in Walton High Street was used as the M/T Store and for petrol; the Ration Store and Pioneer Shop were in Central Avenue and the Regimental Police were located at *Clarendon Villa* in Kirby Road, Walton.

First World War soldier recalled to arms, Home Guardsman Percy Swan in full action dress 1941.
Gertrude Prince

Besides the Brigade's attached units of artillery and logistics, when required the Brigade Commander could also call upon the local Home Guard units in the area: the 9th Battalion Essex Home Guard, which had its HQ at *Weeley House*, Weeley.

The 'Walton Company', under Major Gillett MC, had two Platoons: The Walton & Frinton Platoon, consisting of a Frinton Section and a Walton Section; and The Kirby Platoon, with Sections from Great Holland, Kirby Cross and Kirby–le–Soken.

Although the Home Guard was poorly equipped when hurriedly formed in the summer of 1940, the following year saw an organised force with appropriate arms and equipment *(left).*

Tuesday, 23 July

At about 2 p.m. a dog exploded a defence land mine on Frinton seafront. The blast broke windows at *The Queen's Hotel* and *Thalassa* on The Esplanade.

Wednesday, 24 July

In the early afternoon an unusual discovery was of three balloons which had come down near Walton Pier. At first they were thought to be meteorological balloons but that was later discounted. Two of them were recovered and handed to Walton Police. They were found to contain leaflets in two foreign languages.

Sunday, 28 July

During the early hours of the morning, warning was received in the local area of the possibility of enemy airmen at large, after an enemy aircraft had crashed near Wivenhoe. Later in the morning the warning was cancelled when the airmen were found dead in the wreckage of their aircraft, a Junkers Ju88.

Wednesday, 6 August

Late in the evening reports came in that an aircraft had crashed into the sea off Walton and burst into flames. The location varied from half a mile off the end of the Pier to near the north–east end of the Gunfleet Sands. The lifeboat was ordered to launch and conduct a search. An hour and a half later it was recalled, the Coxswain reporting having seen only oil and smashed timber, but no survivors.

At the same time as the Walton incident, another aircraft was reported down, half a mile off Clacton Pier. On the pier itself, Clacton Coastguards found what they believed to be part of an aircraft's wing, of German origin, and which was thought to have come from the aircraft. Some confusion set in when the Clacton lifeboat reported the position of the aircraft crash as the East Shipwash Buoy, some 12 miles off the Naze. The situation remained unclear thereafter.

Monday, 11 August

At about 7.30 in the morning, the explosion of defence land mines at Frinton seafront caused minor damage to a couple of houses on The Esplanade.

Monday, 18 August

Shortly before midday, a barrage balloon was seen in the sea 3 miles north–east of the Naze.

Wednesday, 3 September

The band and bugles of 5th D.C.L.I. 'Beat Retreat' in Connaught Avenue, Frinton.

Tuesday, 16 September

At 1.54 in the morning, Coastguard Watchman Parsons saw a white light flash out to sea towards the south–south–east, at a range he estimated to be about 3 miles. At 2.12 a.m. the naval authorities ordered the lifeboat to launch, as news had been received of a bomber down in that direction. Just after 4 a.m. the Clacton Coastguards also reported a light on the surface, 3 miles south–east of Clacton and the lifeboat was despatched to that position. An hour later the lifeboat crew reported that both positions had been searched with no result and that they had spoken with a trawler which had seen nothing either. The lifeboat returned, being ready for service again at 7 a.m.

Just after midday there was another report of an aircraft down in the sea 2 miles south–east of Holland–on–Sea. This time the Clacton lifeboat was able to pick up the crew of three from a twin engined Blenheim aircraft which had crashed while outbound from R.A.F. Manston in Kent.

Wednesday, 17 September

The air raid siren had not long sounded when just before 9 p.m. one high–explosive bomb was reported at Ashes Farm, between Walton and Kirby. No damage was reported from the incident, which broke a period of over two months with no bombing activity in the District.

Saturday, 20 September

H.M. Trawler *Marconi* sank after a collision approximately 8 miles east–north–east of the Naze.

Sunday, 21 September

The tanker *Vancouver* was mined and sank approximately 9 miles east of the Naze.

At 10.40 p.m., during an evening air raid alert, two parachute mines fell near Sandy Point, between Frinton and Holland Haven. Reported damage was limited to broken windows and minor damage to eight properties.

Wednesday, 1 October

During the early evening the band of the 5th D.C.L.I. 'Beat Retreat' at Prince's Esplanade, Walton.

Wednesday, 8 October

Minor damage was reported to a house in Westbury Road, Great Holland, after practice gunfire from local artillery.

Saturday, 11 October

At 8.15 p.m., four high–explosive bombs fell on Walton marshes, one causing damage to a seawall. Five minutes later the air raid siren sounded and remained in force for almost the next two hours.

Sunday, 12 October

In the morning, the 5th D.C.L.I. held a Drumhead Service on the carpark at Walton. Later, at the Naze, members of the 5th D.C.L.I. witnessed three Tomahawk fighter aircraft demonstrate dive bombing and, of particular interest to them, low level attack and hedge hopping.

Saturday, 25 October

The air raid siren sounded at 7 p.m. and twenty minutes later four high–explosive bombs fell on Walton marshes.

Monday, 17 November

An air raid alert began at 7.25 p.m. Half an hour later, two parachute mines landed at Eton Road, Frinton. One did not explode but the blast from the other severely damaged six houses and caused lesser damage to over fifty others in the surrounding area. Twelve houses had to be evacuated and twelve people had to be found alternative accommodation. Six people were slightly injured.

On 17th November 1941 the blast from a parachute mine severely damaged properties in Eton Road, Frinton. The photograph below shows damage to, what is believed to be, the rear of *Craigard* (at the junction of Eton Road and The Esplanade) later being used for infantry training. *I. W. M. H24967*

Friday, 21 November

5th Battalion D.C.L.I. moved to Dovercourt and were replaced by 4th Battalion D.C.L.I which came from there.

Saturday, 22 November

During the demolition of concrete defence blocks in Frinton, four properties were damaged at the southern end of The Esplanade and in Second Avenue.

Sunday, 7 December

Japan attacked the U.S. Base at Pearl Harbour.

Thursday, 25 December

At 6.30 p.m., incendiary bombs fell on part of Kirby Road, Walton, near the top of the hill by Cole's Lane. Damage was limited to one property, *D'Arcy Lodge*, being used as a military billet at the time and which had tiles broken and damage to a ceiling.

When summarising the local effects of the war much later on, the *East Essex Gazette* reported, "It is believed that Walton is the only place in England on which bombs have fallen on Christmas Day...a shower of incendiaries fell in the Kirby Road district without doing any damage. Children at a party were comforted with the description of the bombs as 'fireworks'."

After this notable event there followed a lull in bombing incidents which was to last until the following summer.

Monday, 29 December

Practice fire from defence guns caused minor damage to a house in Lower Kirby.

Wednesday, 30 December

Late in the evening, defence landmines exploded at Frinton near the end of Queen's Road, but no damage was reported.

1942

Tuesday, 6 January

The *S.S. Norwich Trader* was mined and sank 8 miles east–north–east of the Naze, near Rough Shoal.

Monday, 12 January

After just a brief stay in the Frinton and Walton area, the 4th Battalion D.C.L.I. moved to Colchester Roman Way Camp for a short period and was relieved by the 13th Battalion, Sherwood Foresters. By 1st February the 5th Battalion D.C.L.I. had returned.

Wednesday, 28 January

At 10.20 p.m. an R.A.F. aircraft, believed to have been a twin engined Whitley, was shot down in the sea by gunfire from ships 7 miles north–east of the Naze. A short burst of light anti–aircraft gunfire had been heard; the aircraft dropped recognition signals, one red, one yellow, then thirty seconds later it fell into the sea. Later one survivor and one body were found.

Saturday, 14 – Sunday, 15 February

Just before midnight on Saturday 14th, Walton Coastguards were alerted by the naval authorities to an aircraft down in the sea by the Sunk Head Buoy, 10 miles south–east of Walton. The lifeboat was launched half an hour after midnight and proceeded to the area. On arrival she found H.M. Drifter *Evening Primrose* in the vicinity of the position given, but the drifter's crew had seen no sign of a crashed aircraft. The lifeboat continued on and searched the 'No.4 R.A.F. Rescue Raft' but, finding no one on board, returned to her station and was ready for further duties just before midday.

Later in the afternoon the Clacton lifeboat had a more successful mission when it went to the aid of a Wellington which had come down near the shore between Butlins and Clacton Pier: five died but two were rescued.

Thursday, 26 February

Late in the afternoon, two sea mines were washed ashore at Walton.

Tuesday, 3 March

In the afternoon a conical shaped 'pilot mine' was found on the beach and later in the evening a parachute was found at Holland Haven.

Friday, 6 March

At midday a cylindrical shaped object was washed ashore.

Wednesday, 18 March

Gunfire from defence guns caused minor damage to one house in Walton Road, Kirby–le–Soken.

Thursday, 19 March

At midday four small yellow unexploded bombs were reported at Kirby.

Saturday, 21 March

In the late evening a spherical balloon trailing wires and canisters was adrift.

Sunday, 5 April

In the evening an unexploded bomb was reported at Prospect Park, Great Holland.

Friday, 10 April

In the early morning, an employee of the Essex Catchment Board informed members of the 5th D.C.L.I. that a suspected unexploded bomb lay just a few hundred yards from their Battalion HQ Mess, in one of Rigdon's Farm fields off Kirby Road, Walton. Whether it was dropped that night or at some earlier time was not known.

Tuesday, 14 April

Practice firing of the coastal defence guns at Frinton caused some minor damage to the Grand Hotel (used as military billets) and broken windows at the Beach Hotel.

Wednesday, 15 April

At 8.30 in the morning, the 5th Battalion D.C.L.I. marched out of Walton for Dovercourt. This time they did not return but remained at Dovercourt until their next move, in September, which was completely out of the area, to the Isle of Wight. Marching in the opposite direction, from Dovercourt, came the 4th Battalion D.C.L.I. for a second short tour of duty in the Frinton and Walton District.

Thursday, 23 April

Just before 7 p.m., two defence land mines exploded on the cliffs opposite *St Monica's* at Southcliff, Walton. Minor damage was caused to four other properties at Southcliff and windows were broken in the Railway Station Master's office.

Sunday, 26 April

In the early evening, the Walton Observer Corps post reported a barrage balloon or parachute in the sea off the Naze.

In early 1942 the sea horizon from Frinton and Walton was marked by two new permanent structures: H.M. Forts *Rough* and *Sunk Head*. They were two of the Royal Navy's four Sea Forts placed in the outer Thames Estuary, armed with two 3.7-inch anti-aircraft guns and two Bofors guns. Rough's Tower can still be seen today, but Sunk Head Tower was blown-up in 1967 to prevent its use by pirate radio stations.

Above: Rough's Fort under tow before being sunk 7 miles off The Naze. *I. W. M. A23870*

Below: One of the other forts in the process of being sunk in position. *I. W. M. A26877*

Thursday, 30 April

At 7.25 a.m. there was a further explosion of defence land mines.

Monday, 18 May

At 4.50 p.m., a Spitfire from 111 Squadron, piloted by Sergeant Hollingdale, made a forced landing at Frinton.

Earlier in the afternoon at R.A.F. Debden, in north–west Essex, Spitfires from 111 Squadron had taken off as part of a Wing formation bound for a 'fighter sweep' over Gravelines near Calais. Take off was at 16.00 hours. The Squadron's diary records that, 'the weather was very unsuitable with thick cloud from 7,000 to about 16,000 feet and the Wing became split up'. Climbing through 8,000 feet, the Spitfires flown by Sergeants Hollingdale and Hetherington, collided.

Sergeant Hollingdale's aircraft suffered a badly damaged propeller. He turned for home and made the coast at Frinton where he successfully force–landed his Spitfire behind the Tennis Courts. He survived the experience without serious injury, although his aircraft was badly damaged. After relating his story he was taken to the nearby Officers' Training School, set up at *Hillcrest* in Second Avenue as part of 45 Division's 'Battle School'.

The Army immediately alerted the Coastguards at Walton that a second Spitfire pilot may have baled out over the sea and the lifeboat was launched at 4.52 p.m. Sergeant Hollingdale estimated that the collision had taken place some 10 to 20 miles off the coast and on a reciprocal bearing from his inward flight, which put the position somewhere between Sunk Head and north of the Kentish Knock in the outer part of the Thames Estuary. The lifeboat was instructed to conduct a search on the bearing of 110 degrees magnetic. Additionally the naval authorities despatched a rescue launch from Harwich and four more from Brightlingsea.

After the suddenness of the collision, Sergeant Hetherington had found his aircraft in an inverted dive and completely out of control. At only about 2,000 feet he was able to bale out and landed safely in the water. His dinghy functioned perfectly and he was able to scramble aboard and await rescue, which fortunately was not long in coming. After half an hour he was picked up by a trawler whose crew had seen him bale out.

Not long afterwards, Walton Coastguards were instructed by the Navy at Harwich to get the lifeboat to head for the trawler at the outer end of the Barrow Deep, some 10 miles south–south–east of Frinton. The message was also relayed to the other search craft and it was an R.A.F. launch that went alongside the trawler and took off Sergeant Hertherington. The Squadron's diary continues that, 'He was taken in to Felixstowe and returned to Debden the next day none the worse. He has now been elected to the Caterpillar Club.'

The Caterpillar Club was run by the Irvin Parachute Company and membership was granted to all those whose lives had been saved by parachute after having been forced to vacate their aircraft. There were, and still are, many members.

Thursday, 28 May

The 4th Battalion D.C.L.I. returned again to Dovercourt and their place was taken by a new unit to the District, the 5th Battalion Somerset Light Infantry.

Thursday, 4 June

In the early morning, just after 3.30 a.m., the naval authorities at Harwich ordered the lifeboat to be launched to search for an aircraft reported down in the sea just south of the Cork Sands. By 4.20 a.m. the lifeboat and boarding boat were away. Both boats searched until six in the morning, when they were recalled by the naval authorities. The Coxswain reported that the area had been searched widely, but no trace of an aircraft or wreckage had been found.

Thursday, 11 June

Further damage was caused by an estimated 18 defence land mines exploding on the Frinton seafront just after 9 p.m. Minor damage was caused to properties in The Esplanade between Oxford Road and The Crescent – *Red Gables, Carlotta, Cambridge House, Frinton Lodge, Turret Lodge* and *Bentley Lodge*; also at the seaward end of Raglan Road – *Nelmes Cottage* and *Raglan House;* and *The Corners* in The Crescent. Further along The Esplanade there was minor damage to *Suffolk House* and windows were broken at the *Queen's Hotel, Willowdene* and *The Cedars.*

To date, every house on The Esplanade north of Connaught Avenue had suffered some form of damage from the detonation of defence mines, some more than once.

Thursday, 13 August

The lull in bombing activity in the District came to an end at 3.15 a.m. when seven high–explosive bombs and an estimated 200 incendiaries fell between Kirby–le–Soken and Frinton. Five of the bombs were the smaller 50kg type, but the other two were large 500kg bombs. Two of the bombs did not explode immediately but had delayed action fuses. Being concentrated in the farm land between Kirby and Frinton, damage to property was only of a minor nature and there were no casualties.

The greatest concentration of property damage was in Frinton. Twenty one houses in Witton Wood Road and five more in the Upper Avenues were affected. Elsewhere the damage was patchy and broadly contained along the boundary roads of Elm Tree Avenue, Kirby Road to Devereux Farm and Turpin's Lane to Frinton Road. In total, 50 houses were slightly damaged, not including those with just broken windows.

The incendiaries caused a number of fires in the fields near *Turpin's Farm,* which were tackled by the residents of the farm's two cottages until help arrived and most of the crop was saved. The unexploded bombs lay close to *Turpin's Farm Cottages.* The next day they detonated and damage was caused to both cottages, displacing or breaking practically all the tiles to the front of the cottages and a good many at the back. The roofs of the farm buildings suffered similarly.

'Germans' and Russians at Frinton and Walton.
The 45th Divisional Battle School based at Frinton had its share of official visitors. On 30th October 1942 a camerman accompanied a visit by the influential Peruvian journalist Senor Emilio Delboy.
Above: During 'house clearance' training (believed to be at *Craigard*, Frinton). Senor Delboy talks to participants in the activities, some dressed as the enemy. *I.W.M. H24969*
Below: Whilst at the Naze exercise area, Senor Delboy (centre) met members of a Russian Military Mission who were paying an unexpected visit. Behind the party, to the right, is the Naze 'decoy site' – small huts that could be ignited at night to divert bombers away from their intended targets. This and another site at Birch Hall, Kirby, served Harwich: the layout of the two sites with the Backwaters in between, probably intended to reflect Felixstowe, the River Stour and Harwich. *I.W.M. H24960*

In 1942 Frinton was home to the 45th Division's 'Battle School' - a continuation training organisation for units within the Division. The School's Staff Officers' Mess was the Golf Clubhouse.

The training was primarily tactics at Platoon or Section level and towards the end of each course, set piece manoeuvres were carried out; the site for one of which was at the Naze cliffs.

Present Frinton resident, Reg Madge, was then a junior officer with 171 Field Regiment, Royal Artillery, which was attached to 45 Division. The unit had three batteries of '25 pounder' field guns, based at Frinton, Thorpe and Clacton. Periodically a troop of guns was required at the Naze to provide realistic artillery fire during the training exercises. The guns were lined against the hedge on the landward perimeter of the golf course, pointing out to sea and they were ranged so the shot fired just above head height as the trainees came over the cliff top.

'Then when at the top, the artillery would open fire.' 45 Division's 'Battle School' training at the Naze cliffs. *I. W. M. H24660*

Reg Madge saw the operation from both sides, for in the autumn of 1942 he was detached from his gun battery to one of the courses. The set piece exercise for his class took place at the Naze golf course cliffs. The start point involved wading out to the seaward side of the defensive line of beach scaffolding then making their way back through it to reach the cliff foot. Sections of cliff were cordoned off for the trainees to climb, while instructors let off explosive 'thunderflashes' for noise effect and fired live rounds over the climbers heads. Once at the top the artillery opened fire. The group then turned right and made their way down the natural ground slope towards the low cliffs and Tarmarisk seawall to their objective. On the way, lines of barbed wire obstacles had to be crossed and the artillery began to fire over their heads, from behind, in the form of supporting fire for the infantry's advance.

Wednesday, 26 August

An air raid warning 'red' was in force when at 10.45 p.m., four high–explosive bombs fell at the Naze close to the seaward end of Hall Lane. One bomb remained unexploded, but the others caused widespread damage and three slight casualties. Just like the incident of 13th November 1940, the vicinity of Harper's Tennis Courts took the full force of the explosions.

The Tennis Court pavilion took a direct hit and was completely destroyed. The nearby home of Mr Harper, *Tennessee*, was so badly damaged that it had to be demolished. The same went for *Mills' Garage* and the Bowling Green club house. On the other side of Hall Lane, between the end of Prince's Esplanade and *Thatched Cottage,* twelve other properties were so severely damaged that some had to be evacuated until repaired: the four bungalows opposite the Tennis Courts (*Sandy Lodge, Court View, Stella Maris* and *Inglethorpe), Gothic Cottage, Clifton Cottages (Nos.1 to 4)* and three empty shops opposite *Mills' Garage.*

Minor damage was inflicted on most properties in the remainder of Hall Lane from *Thatched Cottage* to Naze Park Road and in most of Green Lane, Percival Road and Beatrice Road. Minor damage also extended the full length of East Terrace and included many properties in Saville Street and Standley Road. Isolated pockets of minor damage and broken windows covered an area from Mill Lane and the High Street to the Foundry at the Naze.

Thursday, 3 September

In the morning, a barrage balloon with 200 feet of cable hanging beneath it, was adrift just to the west of Kirby Cross. It was not of the usual type and was thought to have come from a ship.

Thursday, 10 September

At about 11 p.m. a Wellington bomber ditched in the sea, close inshore near Cheveaux de Frise Point, between Holland Haven and Frinton golf course.

No.16 O.T.U. (Operational Training Unit) was based at R.A.F. Upper Heyford and dealt with the final training of Wellington crews before they were posted to operational squadrons. On the night of 10th/11th September the training unit provided a force of 15 Wellingtons to augment a Bomber Command raid on Düsseldorf.

Take off started at just before 8.30 in the evening, but two aircraft failed to take off. During the outward flight the training unit's contribution to the bomber force was further reduced as three other aircraft turned back for various reasons; Wellington R1346, piloted by Sergeant K.J. Johnston, was one of them. The remaining ten aircraft continued on to the target with the main force, but only six made it back to Upper Heyford.

Sergeant Johnston brought 'R1346' back as far as the Essex coast and then ditched the aircraft just offshore, at Cheveaux de Frise Point. Three of the crew survived but two died. The following morning the wreckage of the Wellington, broken in two, could be seen just yards from the shore.

Wellington MkIC, R1346, coded JS–F

Sgt K.J. Johnston	Pilot
Sgt I.F. Leng	Navigator
Sgt A. Boswell	Bomb Aimer
Sgt B.A. Rogers	W.Op/Air Gunner (drowned)
Sgt A.E. Sedin	Air Gunner (missing believed drowned)

Tuesday, 15 September

In the morning a barrage balloon was down in the sea 3 miles north–east of the Naze.

Thursday, 17 September

At 8.45 in the evening an unexploded bomb was reported in the District.

Saturday, 19 September

A dog exploded a defence land mine on the Frinton cliffs causing minor damage to four houses at the seaward end of Pole Barn Lane.

Monday, 28 September

Just after 11 a.m. an enemy aircraft machine–gunned part of Frinton, causing minor damage in Third Avenue, but no casualties.

Previously, just before 11 a.m., a German Dornier Do217 had dropped bombs in Colchester and then on its way out to the coast, had machine–gunned lorries at Weeley, wounding one soldier. It was probably the same aircraft that left its mark on Frinton.

October

By October 1942, 'tip and run' raids by low flying fighter bombers were beginning to make their mark on coastal towns in south and south eastern England. By the first week of October, one Light Anti–Aircraft Troop, consisting of four 40 mm Bofors guns, had been despatched to Walton.

The speed and suddenness of the attacks required the highest state of readiness for the gun crews. To meet that requirement, the order went out that during daylight hours all 40 mm guns deployed within 5 miles of the coast between Lands End and Great Yarmouth, would be manned as follows:

'Skeleton detachments of three men at immediate readiness to engage. Remainder of detachment to stand–to as quickly as possible... One round will be kept on loading tray, rammer to rear and lever foot pedal at hold.'

Saturday, 10 October

An air raid alert began at 7.50 a.m. Twenty minutes later the Bofors light anti–aircraft defences came in to action against a Dornier Do215 bomber, which dropped three or four bombs in the sea 300 yards off the end of Winchester Road at Frinton. Two guns engaged the Dornier, which immediately took avoiding action and made for cloud cover. Twelve properties, scattered widely around and beyond Winchester Road and the end of Pole Barn Lane, reported minor damage after the incident.

Tuesday, 10 November

Six properties along the seafront at Frinton reported minor damage caused by practice gunfire from coastal defence batteries.

Friday, 20 November

Just after 6.30 p.m., a twin engined Beaufighter aircraft crash–landed in the fields south of Holland Hall Farm at Great Holland.

That afternoon No.254 Squadron had carried out its first operational mission using torpedoes. Eleven Beaufighters had taken off from R.A.F. North Coates in Lincolnshire; two were the conventional fighter variant and nine were armed with torpedoes and nick–named 'Torbeaus' by the squadron.

The strike force had set off across the North Sea just after 3 p.m. and an hour later it found a convoy of seven vessels 10 miles off the Dutch coast, which it proceeded to attack. Squadron Leader Sise, flying 'Torbeau' 'R' for Robert, made a torpedo run at the largest vessel of the group. Turning away after the attack, and before the result could be observed, his aircraft was attacked by three Focke–Wulf Fw190 fighters and in the ensuing combat the 'Torbeau' was badly shot–up.

After some effort, Squadron Leader Sise was able to loose his attackers and headed back across the North sea. Landfall was made on the North Essex coast just before 5.45 p.m., but a shortage of fuel meant that Squadron Leader Sise had to put the MkVIC Beaufighter, EL288, down on the nearest suitable piece of land. Both Squadron Leader Sise and his crewman, Flight Sergeant Bibby, were unhurt.

The same day an explosion of unknown origin caused minor damage to 17 properties scattered throughout Frinton and Walton.

Monday, 30 November

During mid morning, a ship's barrage balloon was adrift 4 miles north–east of Walton Pier. It was last seen heading south and descending rapidly until it was lost in the haze when east of the Pier.

Tuesday, 8 December

Defence land mines exploded on the cliffs at Walton, causing minor damage to 13 properties and broken windows in over 40 others. The damage was concentrated along Woodberry Way and The Parade, from Southview Drive to the Pier Hotel.

Tuesday, 22 December

Without warning, just before 10 a.m., two high–explosive bombs and ten 'firepots' fell at Holland Haven. No damage or casualties were reported.

Sunday, 27 December

In the late morning, the sailing barge *Gertrude May* was blown–up in the Wallet, some 2 miles off the Frinton golf course. The naval authorities at Brightlingsea ordered the lifeboat to launch, which it did just before 11.30. While the lifeboat was on its way to the scene, another sailing barge picked up the skipper of the stricken vessel and later transferred him to a rescue boat from Brightlingsea. There was no trace of the other crew member so the lifeboat was recalled.

1943

Monday, 4 January

An air raid alert was in force for an hour during the evening and minor damage was reported to a house in Hall Lane, Walton, as a result of anti–aircraft gunfire.

Wednesday, 6 January

No sooner had the air raid alarm been sounded at 2.40 p.m., when an enemy aircraft flew over and machine–gunned part of the Kirby Road, damaging roof tiles and slates at *Brick Barn* farm buildings, Kirby–le–Soken.

Tuesday, 12 January

The explosion of a defence land mine caused broken windows in a house at Woodberry Way, Walton.

Saturday, 23 January

Minor roof damage was reported to *Dairy House* farm buildings in Great Holland, thought to have been the result of anti–aircraft gunfire.

Sunday, 24 January

The detonation of defence land mines on Frinton Cliffs again caused damage to properties along The Esplanade, between Connaught Avenue and Queen's Road. This time the damage was limited to broken windows at *The Queen's Hotel, Apple Trees, The Bungalow* and *Yarra.*

Thursday, 28 January

The barge *Resolute,* of Mistley, was on passage from London to Ipswich with a cargo of wheat. Just before midday she struck a mine about a mile south of Holland Haven. The Clacton lifeboat, being nearest the scene, was despatched and managed to launch in just eight minutes, by not waiting for a full crew. Another barge rescued the skipper of the Resolute and transferred him to the lifeboat when it arrived.

Saturday, 30 January

A barrage balloon was adrift over Kirby during the morning, just one of a number reported over the coastal area at that time.

Tuesday, 2 February

Men of the 2nd/7th Warwickshire Regiment arrived in Frinton from Northern Ireland for a two month stay, during which time they were to take part in Division and Brigade exercises in the local area.

Thursday, 4 February

Between 9 p.m. and 10 p.m., an aircraft was seen to come down in the sea between Frinton and Holland–on–Sea. Earlier in the evening, at Weeley, two parachute mines had been dropped; one close to the church exploded at 8.20, but the other remained unexploded. There was no air raid warning in force and whether the two incidents were related is not clear.

Friday, 5 February

In the morning the Coastguards reported an aircraft in the sea south of Frinton, off Holland Haven. Earlier a damaged German dinghy had been found off Frinton. It is very probable that these discoveries were related to the previous evening's incident.

Wednesday, 17 February

Nearby Clacton became the target of a 'tip and run' raid when at breakfast time, low flying Focke-Wulf Fw190's bombed the town, causing damage to property and casualties.

Wednesday, 24 – Thursday, 25 February

182 Infantry Brigade's 'Exercise Wire' took place in the Frinton and Walton area.

Saturday, 27 February

At 6 p.m. the watchman at the Naze Auxiliary Coastguard Lookout Station reported a man cut off by the tide at the Swatchway, Stone Point. The Coastguard District Officer, Station Officer and two Auxiliary Coastguards made their way to the scene with line throwing gear and life lines. As they approached, the man, a Czech soldier, waded across unaided.

Sunday, 14 March

In the early afternoon at eleven minutes past two, what were believed to have been six Focke–Wulf Fw190 fighter–bombers, suddenly appeared over Frinton and Walton. Low and fast, they machine gunned the area and dropped six high–explosive bombs: three at Frinton, two at Walton and one at Lower Kirby. No sooner had the attack begun than it was over, leaving six dead, fourteen injured and a number of houses destroyed and many more damaged. A rescue party, two first aid parties and two ambulances were sent from Clacton to assist the local organisations.

At Kirby, the high–explosive bomb landed near Turpin's Lane, damaging two houses.

At Frinton, one high–explosive bomb exploded near the railway crossing, causing a number of injuries, but none serious. Not too far away a 250kg high–explosive bomb lay unexploded in the living room of a house in Green Way, half way between Old Parsonage Way and St Mary's Road.

A Fock-Wulf Fw190 fighter bomber, of the type used in the 'tip and run' raids. *Chris Goss*

The third bomb in Frinton destroyed an unoccupied house in Fourth Avenue and damaged two others being used as billets by the 2nd/7th Warwickshire Regiment. Two of their soldiers were killed – Privates C.H. Gibson and N. Hall – and a third was injured by shrapnel, but not seriously. Four Army trucks were extensively damaged in the explosion and two soldiers were admitted to hospital. The men of the Warwickshire Regiment were only in the town temporarily for exercises and the day before they had just completed a ten day 'Exercise Spartan', the latest in a series during their stay in the area. Two weeks later the battalion moved on from Frinton.

At Walton, two bombs were reported in the vicinity of the Round Gardens and Station Street, but damage was concentrated in one locality: at the end of The Crescent where it turns into New Pier Street. There a row of four cottages and a shop were destroyed, killing lifeboatman George Aldrich and his wife, an elderly neighbour Mrs Saint and 83 year old Mr Harrison. One other person was admitted to hospital and three others slightly injured. The bomb that caused the damage had landed first in Grant's coal yard by the railway station (possibly the intended target); it ricocheted, struck the base of a crane and was deflected to its final point of impact.

The Congregational Church Hall Rest Centre was opened at Walton for nine people made homeless until they were found alternative accommodation. In Frinton, 150 people were evacuated while the unexploded bomb in Green Way was dealt with.

The attack had been without warning, short lived and damaging: a typical 'tip and run' raid. Neighbouring Clacton had been hit in a similar manner a month earlier. The attack was significant for the casualties that resulted, but also, after nearly four years of war and numerous bombing incidents, it was the first time that Frinton and Walton had been specifically singled out as targets for attack. It was not to be the only occasion.

Thursday, 18 March

The air raid alert was in force four times during the day, but never for more than 15 or 20 minutes at a time. The last alert began at 10.30 in the evening and this time gunfire from the anti–aircraft batteries resulted in minor damage to 13 houses in Frinton: 8 in Pole Barn Lane and the remainder in Eton Road and Winchester Road.

Walton C 10

1	2	3	4	5	6
Walton	51° 50′ N 1° 16′ O	20 m	acht 70 u. 60 m hohe Funkmasten, 110 m über NN, 14,5 km WNW von Walton	Nr. 30	**C 10**
The Naze	51° 52′ N 1° 18′ O				

Entfernungen von the Naze:

North Foreland 56 km   Dünkirchen 118 km

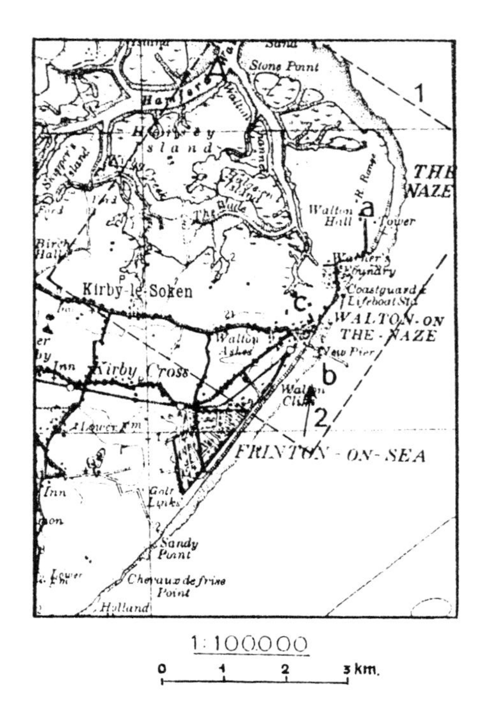

Walton-on-the-Naze ist ein 3100 Einwohner großer Badeort, 3 km SSW der niedrigen, stumpfwinkligen Huk **the Naze,** die sich in einer niedrigen Kliffküste nach S über Walton hinaus fortsetzt. 3 km NW der Huk mündet das weitverzweigte Hamford-Water (A), dessen Mündung ein 2,5 km breiter Wattenstreifen vorgelagert ist, der nach S schnell an Breite abnimmt (vor the Naze 250 m breit, vor Walton 200 m breit). 1 km südlich folgt der Badeort Frinton (2200 Einw.).

Besondere Merkmale sind:

b) die 850 m lange Landebrücke mit nach S umgebogenem Kopf,

c) ein Stauteich nördlich des Ortes.

A page from a 1943 Luftwaffe air navigation guide to Great Britain.

Courtesy of Frinton & Walton Heritage Trust

Wednesday, 31 March

Just after midday the naval authorities at Brightlingsea instructed the lifeboat to launch and proceed to the vicinity of Long Sand, some 12 miles south–east of Walton, where there were four airmen in the water from a crashed aircraft. The lifeboat searched the position and returned at 7 p.m. having found nothing.

Thursday, 15 April

Shrapnel from anti–aircraft gunfire caused minor damage to one house in Walton and another in Kirby.

Saturday, 17 April

The *S.S. Dynamo* was mined and sank 11 miles east of Walton.

Sunday, 30 May

At twenty five minutes past seven in the evening, a second 'tip and run' raid was made against Frinton and Walton, causing further civilian casualties and much damage in the towns. Again the strike was made by Fw190 fighter–bombers; the exact number being unclear, but probably ten in all, in what was to become the District's most damaging raid of the war.

Again the aircraft approached low and fast, coming in over the sea to the south of Frinton, then after crossing the coast, turning north–east to run over Frinton and Walton from a landward direction. Twenty high–explosive bombs were recorded as falling between Frinton's Avenues and the Naze. No air raid warning 'red' had been received at the A.R.P. Control Centre and the bombs began to fall before the siren was sounded. The attack lasted no more than a minute and was made at roof top level; so low that many of the bombs did not detonate on first impact, but ricocheted and exploded where they touched ground a second time.

Seven bombs fell in Frinton. *The Beach Hotel,* near the corner of Third Avenue and The Esplanade, took a direct hit and was effectively cut in half, leaving the lift shaft protruding from the rubble. The *East Essex Gazette* reporter described the building as, "looking as if a giant had clawed a piece out of the centre". The proprietor, Mr Homer, was on the top floor at the time and had to await rescue by the Civil Defence Rescue Party. The manageress, Miss Smith and a friend were both injured and needed hospital treatment.

Nearby on the Greensward, seventeen year old Home Guardsman Ken Haggis was on guard duty at the coastal defence gun battery opposite the *Grand Hotel.* (The Frinton & Walton Company of the Home Guard had recently taken over much of the responsibility for manning the battery from the Royal Artillery 'regulars'.) He saw the bomb from one aircraft fall immediately in front of the *Grand Hotel.* It struck and demolished a small boundary wall and two 'rocket guns' parked just outside, before ricocheting over the neighbouring building (being used as a billet for soldiers manning the coastal gun battery) and landing on the other side of the 'Gun Garden' at the

Bomb impact points and explosions, Frinton 30th May 1943.

Based on a 1938 Ordnance Survey Map, courtesy of Essex Record Office

bottom of Connaught Avenue, demolishing the house *Forres*. A cloud of red dust from the remains of *Forres,* drifted back towards the gun battery and as the soldiers spilled out of their billet an instinctive cry went up of 'gas! gas!', until the source of the cloud was realised.

The small Church of St Mary's, on the opposite side of the Gun Garden, had most of its windows broken, as did the Free Church further along Connaught Avenue, where a service was in progress, but there were no casualties amongst the congregation.

After dropping its load, Ken Haggis saw the Fw190 turn to head out to sea, but as it did so another aircraft came from further inland, slightly higher and with the same intention. As the two aircraft met, the lower one effectively ran out of air space and crashed into the sea.

Three other bombs fell in various parts of Frinton's Third Avenue. One fell between *The Den* and its neighbouring house, wrecking both. At *The Den,* one side of the house collapsed and Mr Kingsman, Miss Kingsman and Mrs Bowerman were all subsequently taken to hospital. A second bomb fell on the opposite side of the road and a third fell further along Third Avenue, bouncing twice in front gardens on the west side of the road, before exploding at its third point of impact half way between the Holland Road junction and Ashlyn's Road.

Another 'bouncing' bomb struck first in the back garden of one of the semi–detached houses in Old Road, just to the north of the church, then flew over the remaining back gardens in the road and exploded in Connaught Avenue, opposite *Ratcliffe's Garage.* A fire broke out next door at *Race and Scott's* stables, but it was quickly extinguished and the horses were saved. On the other side of the road a bungalow, being used as Civil Defence Rescue Depot Offices, was destroyed and Civil Defence Ambulance Driver, Mr Griggs, was critically injured and later died. A married man, he had been in the Army during the early part of the war, but had been invalided out and had been in the Civil Defence for the previous two years.

The final bomb in the Frinton area struck the water tower by the railway line, but then continued its flight a further thousand yards to land between the bungalows *Lynton* and *Greenlea* in Elm Tree Avenue. *Lynton* was demolished, but the occupants had managed to get into their makeshift Morrison shelter, from which Mrs Wyatt was rescued, injured, together with her mother and year old baby. Next door, *Greenlea* was severely damaged, but fortunately the occupants were away at the time.

Between Frinton and Walton a single bomb landed in the fields just behind the houses by the entrance to Cole's Lane off Kirby Road; it 'bounced' and landed two thousand yards further down the lane in open farm land.

Five bombs fell in the town of Walton, all on the Frinton side. One, by the first bend in the Walton Road past the church, remained unexploded, causing the road to be closed and nearby residents to be evacuated until it was dealt with. Another bomb impacted further along the Walton Road, then 'bounced' and came to rest by the bungalows opposite the cemetery. Without bouncing, another bomb made a direct hit on *The Briars* in Kirby Road. Mrs Smith and her two daughters Elsie and Florence,

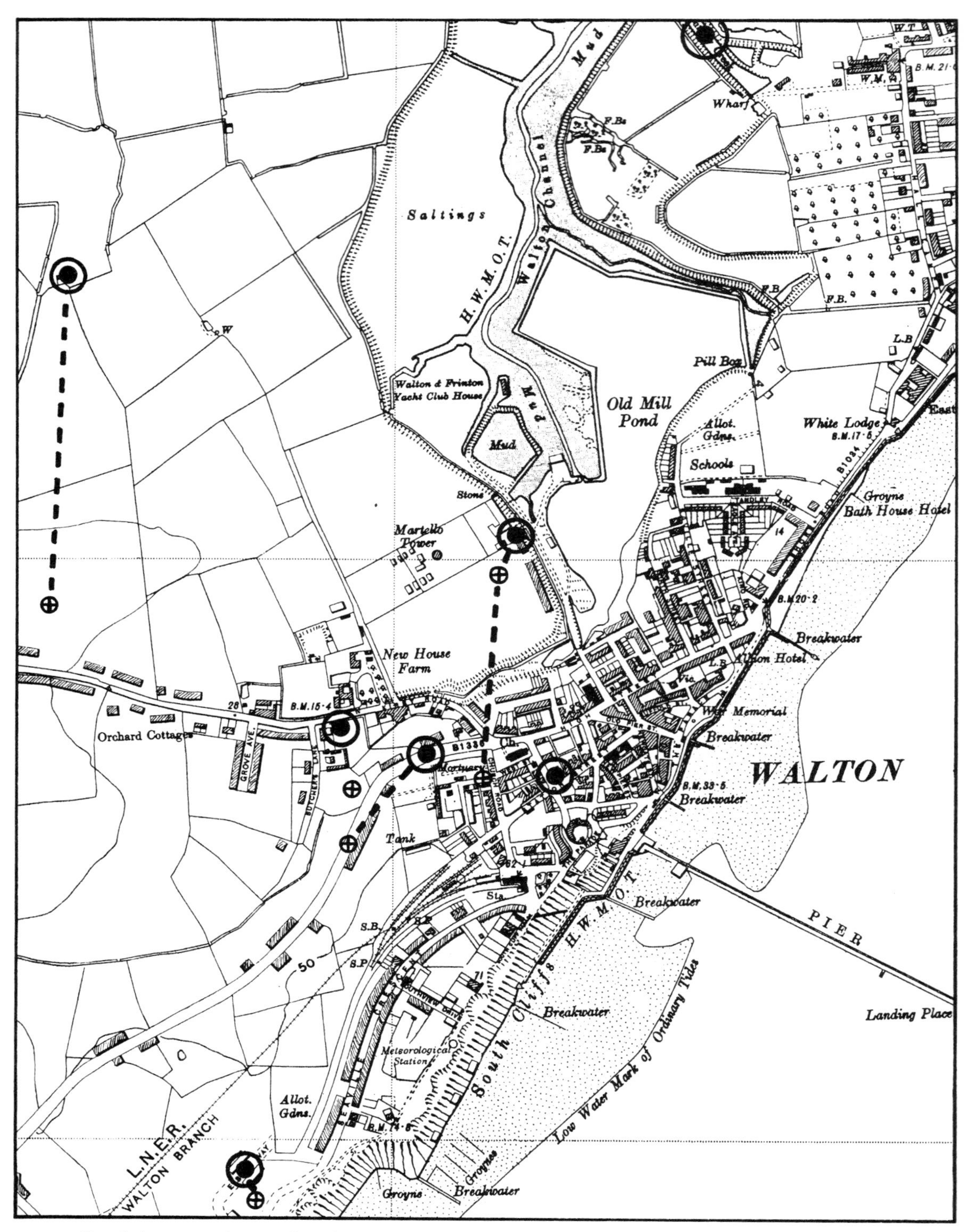

Bomb impact points and explosions, Walton 30th May 1943.

Based on a 1938 Ordnance Survey Map, courtesy of Essex Record Office

were killed and Mr Smith, who had been in the garden, was severely injured and taken to hospital. It is believed that a soldier on the pavement opposite was also killed.

The Catholic Church, at the corner of Martello Road and Station Street, was demolished by a direct hit, along with an adjacent house in Martello Road. Next to it the Police Station was damaged to such a degree that for the remainder of the war temporary premises had to be used. Police Sergeant Dorkin received a commendation for his actions that evening.

The other bomb to cause damage in the town, struck the boundary wall of the house at the bottom of Church Road, opposite the cemetery, ricocheted into the camping ground behind the houses in Mill Lane and then on into the last house in Mill Lane: *Riverside,* the home of Major and Mrs Cripps. The house was destroyed and Mrs Nona Cripps was killed. The *East Essex Gazette* report at the time described how Mrs Cripps (the head of the Walton Red Cross) had been upstairs in her home resting having been unwell. When rescuers reached her she was unconscious and minutes later she died. Major Cripps was in the garden at the time and had a miraculous escape.

At the Naze, a bomb fell in the vicinity of Foundry Creek while three more fell closer to the Naze Tower. One struck the fields on the opposite side of Hall Lane to the *Samuel Lewis Convalescent Home,* bounced over the road and demolished the north wing of the Home. The second, hit the top of the cliffs close to the most northerly pillbox on the cliff edge, bounced over the edge and exploded on the foreshore, close to where the third exploded just a few hundred yards north of Tower Breakwater. A fourth bomb was believed to have exploded about a mile out to sea off the Naze.

In such a short period, the twenty bombs resulted in six dead and twenty one injured, of which ten were sent to Clacton Hospital. The electricity transformer station at Walton had been put out of action and gas and electricity services were damaged at three locations and the sewers at one. Six houses had been demolished, twenty were severely damaged and hundreds slightly damaged. To date it had been the single most damaging raid of the war in the District.

At the time there were claims that two or three of the raiders had been shot down, but as already described, one of them had been the result of a near collision, verified later in the A.R.P. reporting of the incident. Certainly at Frinton the Bofors anti–aircraft gun near the golf course did not open fire until the raiders were heading back out to sea again. A second aircraft was believed to have come down in the sea off the Naze, but it is more than likely that the splash observed was the result of a bomb burst.

The lifeboat was launched at ten past eight and proceeded to investigate the crashed aircraft off Frinton. Frank Bloom, later to become Lifeboat Coxswain, was home on leave from the Royal Navy and went out with the lifeboat crew. Close inshore they found the body of Feldwebel [Sergeant] Fritz Kessler supported by his life jacket. Either he had been thrown clear during the impact or, more likely, he had survived the unexpected ditching and had managed to undo his straps and extricate himself from the cockpit only to succumb when in the water.

The lifeboat returned with Fritz Kessler's body to Walton Pier, but immediately was directed to the second position a few hundred yards off the Naze. Nothing was found before other Service vessels arrived to take up the search and the lifeboat returned to her moorings. It is believed that nothing was ever found and in all probability what was thought to have been an aircraft crashing was most likely a bomb exploding in the sea.

Anti–aircraft gunners' claims might have had some substance though, as one pilot, Leutnant [Pilot Officer] Alois Harlos, soon discovered smoke coming from his engine as he headed out to sea. He was not sure if it was the result of damage inflicted by the ground defences or just a mechanical fault; the cause did not matter, but the effect did. He flew on in the hope that he would reach the Belgian coast, but after what must have been 30 or 40 miles, his engine stopped with a severe jerk.

As in the outward journey, he had been flying low over the sea to avoid detection. As soon as the raid had been identified, R.A.F. fighters had been scrambled to cut off the 'nine plus' raiders reported as heading out to sea. Harlos tried to gain some height but only reached 300 feet, which was far too low to bale out. The alternative was to ditch and as the sea was unusually calm it became the preferred option and was achieved successfully. Once down, Harlos scrambled into his rubber dinghy and began the wait for whatever fate had in store for him. He was fortunate that the sea remained calm during the night, so much so that under the clear starlight he was treated to a display of bio–luminescence in the water.

The following day the wind began to pick up and the sea responded. In the afternoon, after a group of twin engined 'Mitchell' light bombers had attacked a target in Flushing, one of them was forced to ditch in the sea not far from the English coast and the crew was picked up by a high speed launch (H.S.L.). Further out, one of the bombers' escorting Spitfires, from 402 Squadron, had come down in the sea and the Air Sea Rescue Flight at Martlesham Heath was alerted.

A Walrus seaplane was despatched to the position, along with two Spitfires. Arriving first, the two Spitfires from the Air Sea Rescue Flight, found three other 402 Squadron aircraft circling the dinghy containing their colleague. Unfortunately the Air Sea Rescue Walrus, piloted by Warrant Officer Tommy Ormiston, had developed a radio problem and had to resort to basic 'dead reckoning' navigation to locate the search area. Arriving at what was estimated to have been the position, there was nothing to be seen. Meanwhile, another Walrus was despatched for the downed Spitfire pilot who eventually was picked up by an H.S.L.

Warrant Officer Ormiston made a brief search of the area he had arrived at and when just turning for home, spotted an airman in a dinghy waving his arms. A smoke float was dropped to check the wind conditions and then Warrant Officer Ormiston put the Walrus down on the sea to pick up an unexpected, but thankful German airman. Earlier in the day Leutnant Harlos had heard aircraft flying to and fro in the direction of the coast, but too far away to see. Later he thought he had been seen by some Spitfires and that their sighting had brought out the Walrus, but it was not quite like that. How it happened did not matter, the Walrus was a most welcome sight after a full 24 hours in the rubber dinghy!

The grateful Harlos (at the age of thirty four, somewhat older than most pilots) was taken aboard for the flight back to Martlesham Heath, where his injuries were attended to at the Station's sick quarters. The next day he was escorted to London for the inevitable interrogation before onward despatch to a prisoner of war camp.

At Walton, the body of twenty three year old Fritz Kessler was taken to the mortuary and later buried in the local cemetery. After the war the body was re–interred at the German War Cemetery at Cannock Chase. As far as is known, only two Fw190's were lost during the raid, both type 'A5 U8' from SKG10 (Schnellkampfgeschwader, or 'fast bomber group'10) based at Koksijde in Belgium:

Lt. Alois Harlos – 7/SKG10, Fw190 No.0824, coded yellow 'H'.
Feldw. Fritz Kessler – 5/SKG10, Fw190 No.0910, coded white 'L'.

Wednesday, 2 June

One high–explosive bomb caused minor damage to three properties in Kirby.

Wednesday, 23 June

At 6.35 p.m., the Coastal Gun Battery at Frinton informed the Walton Coastguards that an aircraft was down in the sea 1½ miles from them on a bearing of 200 degrees – making it in the Wallet, to the north of the Gunfleet Sands, just off Holland Haven. At the same time the Observer Corps had reports of a Flying Fortress down in the sea 1½ miles south of the Gunfleet Sands: a splash had been seen, followed by smoke.

The lifeboat was launched at 8.00 p.m. and proceeded to search, using the motor boarding boat as well. After an hour they were recalled, the Coxswain reporting nothing seen or found.

Friday, 9 July

During the evening the Sailing Barge *Maria* got into difficulties about 5 miles south of Clacton, near the Spitway – a shallow and variable channel between the Gunfleet and Buxey Sands. The R.N.L.I. report continues:

"While bound from Rochester to Maldon with a load of brick rubble, the barge *Maria,* of Rochester, lost her sprit and was in difficulties about one and a half miles south–west of the Swin Spit bell buoy. A light south–west wind was blowing, with a rough sea. The Clacton–on–Sea lifeboat was launched at 7.39 p.m., but her engine broke down, and at 9.40 p.m. the Walton and Frinton lifeboat *E.M.E.D.* was launched to help her, but when it was learned at Walton that she was making for her station under sail, a wireless message was sent to the *E.M.E.D.* to go to the barge instead. She reached her at 11.10 p.m. and stood by her through the night. The barge had two men on board. At about 5 o'clock next morning the life–boat took the barge to Brightlingsea creek, and returned to her station, arriving at 12.42 p.m."

Monday, 16 August

Windows were broken at the Grand Hotel, Frinton, during the demolition of some defence land mines.

Wednesday, 18 August

An air raid alert was in force from the previous evening, and just after midnight twelve high–explosive bombs fell to the south–west of Walton. They were believed to have been small 50kg bombs. There were no casualties and damage to property was only minor: seven houses in Easton Way at Frinton Park Estate, and one each in Walton Road and Woodberry Way. Elsewhere there were isolated cases of a few broken windows.

Saturday, 4 September

Practice for the anti–aircraft gunners required the assistance of aircraft specially designated for the task, either for 'tracking runs' where the gunners would follow the aircraft in their sights, or for target towing during live firings at a 'sleeve target': an open ended fabric tube, rather like an airfield wind–sock, which was streamed at a distance behind the aircraft. The aircraft used for these purposes were usually brightly painted for ease of identification and came from Anti–Aircraft Co–operation (A.A.C.) units. No.1627 (A.A.C.) Flight, was one such unit which had been established at Ipswich Airport, then known as R.A.F. Ipswich.

In the late afternoon of September 4th, a Martinet aircraft, No.MS659 from 1627 (A.A.C.) Flight, was towing a target for the local anti–aircraft gunners when its engine cut out, it stalled and crashed into a field at the Naze, to the west of Walton Hall, killing the Polish pilot, 23 year old Pilot Officer Henryk Wroblewski.

Monday, 6 September

At about 10 p.m. an enemy aircraft was reported down in the sea to the east of Holland–on–Sea.

Small groups of Focke–Wulf Fw190 fighter–bombers were still making nuisance 'tip and run' raids on the south–east coast, now at night as well, thus keeping the anti–aircraft and fighter defences on a constant state of alert.

That evening, 85 Squadron, based at R.A.F. West Malling in Kent, had a twin engined Mosquito aircraft on patrol over the Channel under the control of Sandwich G.C.I. (Ground Control Interception). Squadron Leader Howitt and his Navigator, Flight Lieutenant Houghton, had taken off at 20.35 hours in their night–fighter Mosquito, coded 'VY–Y' and were at 18,000 feet when the G.C.I. informed them of 'trade' to the south.

The heading was followed almost as far as Boulogne until the direction was altered to north–west and at 8,000 feet. Several other 'vectors' followed, generally in a north–westerly direction, until eventually contact was made on the Mosquito's airborne interception radar at a range of 1½ miles. The range was down to 1,000 yards as the two aircraft crossed the coast in the Clacton area, but then the searchlights began to hamper the operation. Flashing the Mosquito's downward recognition lights had no effect on the searchlights, but then cloud cover came to their aid and doused the beams.

Unteroffizier Helmut Breier, missing 6th September 1943
Maria Breier

Closing to just over 300 yards, visual contact was made with the faint glow of the target's exhaust. The enemy aircraft then manoeuvred in a complete circle to the right followed by another circle to the left, then put its nose down and pulled away from the following Mosquito. Levelling out, the enemy aircraft dropped its bombs somewhere in the Ipswich area: the Mosquito's crew observed a bright flash on the ground.

Squadron Leader Howitt then closed right in until he got a clear view of a Focke–Wulf Fw190. He fired a two second burst and strikes were seen on the Fw190's fuselage, followed by a glow, before it went down vertically. Squadron Leader Howitt made a left turn and saw the Fw190 burning on the sea just off Clacton. The time was 21.56.

Gunners at the Holland–on–Sea Coastal Battery site reported a fire on the sea in the distance, towards the east–south–east and recorded it in their log against a time of 21.50 hours.

Unteroffizier Helmut Breier, flying a Focke–Wulf Fw190 A–5, of 1/SKG 10 (Schnellkampfgeschwader or 'fast bomber group' No.10), failed to return from a sortie over the southern North Sea that evening. There is little doubt that all three incidents relate to the same event.

Tuesday, 21 September

During the late afternoon a barrage balloon was adrift offshore between the Naze and Felixstowe.

At 11 p.m. and without an air raid warning, 19 high– explosive bombs fell between Great Holland and Kirby Cross. There were no casualties but damage was widespread. Although mostly of a minor nature, it affected properties in Great Holland from Church Lane and the Little Clacton Road, north through the centre of the village and along Kirby Road to Kirby Cross. There damage was mainly confined to the shops and nearby houses in Frinton Road. Just five minutes later the air raid warning began.

In all just over 100 properties experienced some form of damage other than just broken windows. Two properties suffered more severely. The School in Rectory Road had extensive damage to roof tiles and the rear walls, doors had been forced off their hinges, ceilings badly damaged and numerous windows broken. On the Little Clacton Road, the house *Linzi* had suffered similarly after one bomb had landed just behind it, spattering the walls with shrapnel and badly damaging the fabric of the building.

Saturday, 9 October

Shrapnel from anti–aircraft gunfire caused minor damage to five properties in Walton.

Friday, 15 October

Just before midnight an aircraft was believed to have crashed offshore.

Sunday, 31 October

In the late evening one high–explosive bomb fell in the sea, without causing any damage.

Saturday, 6 November

At 10.50 p.m. during an air raid alert, two high–explosive bombs fell at Great Holland. There were no casualties and minor damage was limited to four properties in Pork Lane and the Little Clacton Road.

Saturday, 13 November

The *S.S. Cormorant* was mined and sank 11 miles east–north–east of Walton.

Saturday, 27 November

The *S.S. Morar,* carrying a cargo of cement, was mined and sank 11 miles east of Walton.

Thursday, 9 December

Between 7 and 7.30 p.m., two unidentified aircraft were seen to crash into the sea off Frinton, one directly offshore in a south–easterly direction and the other towards the south–south–west.

Friday, 10 December

Three houses in Frinton and one in Walton were slightly damaged by shrapnel from anti–aircraft gunfire.

Tuesday, 21 December

A Norwegian ship, the *S.S. Norhaur,* was mined and sank 11 miles off Walton, only a mile from where the *S.S. Morar* had come to grief a month earlier.

1944

Wednesday, 19 January

A 50kg unexploded bomb was found. It was believed to have been one of those dropped during the night of 17th/18th August 1943 when 12 high–explosive bombs fell in the Frinton Park Estate development, between Frinton and Walton.

Friday, 21 January

Gunfire from defence gun batteries caused minor damage to three properties in Frinton.

Saturday, 29 January

Shrapnel from anti–aircraft gunfire caused minor damage to one house in Second Avenue, Frinton and to another in Kirby Road, Walton.

Friday, 4 February

Shrapnel from anti–aircraft gunfire caused minor damage to 11 properties in Frinton, Kirby and Walton.

Saturday, 5 February

Just before 4.30 p.m., an American 'Marauder' aircraft ditched in the sea a mile off Holland Haven. The crew survived and the floating aircraft was taken in tow, but it sank when a mile off Clacton Pier.

Sunday, 13 February

Just before 5.00 p.m., an American fighter crashed into the sea 2 miles off Holland. The Clacton lifeboat was launched but the pilot, Lieutenant Robert Brown of the 357th Fighter Group, was picked up by an Air Sea Rescue launch from Brightlingsea.

The 357th Fighter Group was based at Leiston in Suffolk and this was only their second operational mission since arriving in Britain from the U.S.A.; the first had been just two days previously. This second mission was a 'fighter sweep' over the French coast at Dieppe. The story of Lieutenant Brown's incident is related by Merle Olmsted in his book on the 357th Fighter Group, *"The Yoxford Boys"*.

"On the run back to England, Lt.Robert W. Brown of the 362nd Squadron [of the 357th Fighter Group] became the first of many Group pilots to bail out into the North Sea and to be picked up by the RAF's Air Sea Rescue service.

It was Brown's first mission and he was headed home over the sea at 20,000 feet when things began to happen. With no warning of any kind his engine quit cold and resisted all attempts to start it. The plane descended to 6,000 feet and he went over the side, striking his legs on the tail group as he fell away. His parachute opened and he descended into the water where he bobbed about for 30 minutes before an ASR launch crew pulled him aboard. This was about twice the normal survival time in the cold waters of the North Sea. Soon after pickup he lost consciousness and was to remain in this state for over two weeks. He was taken to a small British coastal hospital [Clacton] where U.S. Army doctors were called in and it was found that his right leg was broken, his left leg badly mangled and that he had contracted pneumonia and was suffering from shock. Although the medical battle took months, Brown did survive the results of his eventful first mission."

During the evening, an air raid alert was in force from 8.20 until 10 p.m. The warning was justified as 27 high–explosive bombs and many incendiaries fell throughout the District. Surrounding areas of Essex were also hit at the same time and Clacton in particular suffered its worst raid of the war as thousands of incendiaries started numerous fires.

In the Frinton and Walton Urban District the damage was relatively light considering the quantity of explosives dropped. Thirty eight properties suffered minor damage, none serious, and there were no casualties. The greatest concentration of damage was to properties between Great Holland and Thorpe Road at Kirby Cross (25) and also at The Street in Kirby–le–Soken (10).

Elsewhere in the District, incidents were more isolated and most of the damage was to roof tiles and slates, ceilings or broken windows. At the Walton Methodist Church the new hole in the roof was not too severe, but it could have been much worse, for beneath it lay a 50kg composite high–explosive and incendiary bomb, which had failed to detonate and spread its fiery load. Nearby on the foreshore, a hole had been gouged out of the Marine Breakwater's masonry, twelve feet by six and three feet deep.

Saturday, 19 February

An aircraft was believed to have crashed in the vicinity of the entrance to Walton Backwaters just before 1 a.m., but there was no confirmation of the incident and nothing more was reported.

Sunday, 20 February

Shrapnel from anti–aircraft gunfire caused minor damage to the roofs of 20 houses spread throughout Frinton and Walton.

Tuesday, 22 February

In the early afternoon, what was believed to be a ship's raft was seen a couple of miles off the Naze, to the east of the Stone Banks Buoy. The lifeboat was launched to investigate, but on arrival found the object to be five timbers tied together with no one on board.

Wednesday, 23 February

Damage was reported to a further 21 properties in Frinton, Kirby and Walton, as a result of anti–aircraft gunfire.

Friday, 25 February

The American 358th Fighter Group (comprising the 365th, 366th and 367th Fighter Squadrons) was based at Raydon in Suffolk, half way between East Bergholt and Hadleigh. On the afternoon of February 25th, the Group had been detailed for an escort mission covering the withdrawal of a formation of B–17 bombers over northern France. Forty-eight P–47 'Thunderbolt' fighters, 16 from each Squadron, were to make up the Group's formation (not including spare aircraft).

Take off was at 14.00 hours for a route that would take them over the southern North Sea to make a landfall at Ostend. At Raydon and over the coast, there was complete cloud cover starting at 2,000 feet and going all the way up to 4,000 feet. Heading out to sea, the formation entered the cloud and once clear, a communications check revealed that 'Red 2', 2nd Lieutenant Carl Shannon, flying Thunderbolt No.42–75175, was missing.

At about the same time, Walton Coastguards reported an aircraft, thought to have been an American 'Thunderbolt', as crashing into the sea in flames, 3 miles to the east of the lookout station. The lifeboat was launched, but all that could be found was a patch of oil on the surface.

The two incidents are very probably related. The Royal Observer Corps later reported the loss of a Raydon based Thunderbolt which had collided with two others. The other two had turned back but the third had crashed into the sea.

Thursday, 2 March

In the early evening, a four engined Liberator aircraft was reported to be down in the sea, at a position some 17 miles south–south–east of Walton, by Fisherman's Gat on Long Sand. Both the Frinton & Walton and Clacton lifeboats were launched to search the area, but nothing was found.

Friday, 3 March

At about 2.30 in the afternoon an allied aircraft, believed to have been a Thunderbolt, crashed at Great Holland immediately to the west of the village.

Saturday, 11 March

General Bernard Montgomery inspected troops at Frinton and Walton.

Friday, 24 March

Sometime after eight in the morning the watchman at the Naze Auxiliary Signal Station, heard cries for help coming from the direction of Pye Sands. At the same time reports of two B–17 'Flying Fortress' bombers having collided and crashed on Pye Sands, were coming in to the Coastguards, the Royal Observer Corps and the R.A.F's. Air Sea Rescue Service. Such an event would mean potentially 20 men in difficulties.

The Lifeboat was launched but was beaten to the scene by a Walrus seaplane from 277 Squadron's Air Sea Rescue Flight at Martlesham Heath. There, word had come in that two Fortresses had collided off Walton–on–the–Naze and were burning on the sea.

Pilot Officer Ormiston, with crew of Warrant Officer Leighton and Sergeant Mullins, in Walrus 3072, were airborne at 8.30 for the short flight to Walton. On arrival they turned on to a north easterly heading and just a mile off shore saw an airman in a dinghy. Pilot Officer Ormiston put the Walrus down on the sea and picked up the survivor, who although wet through appeared little the worse for his experience. The Walrus returned to Martlesham and 2nd Lieutenant Donald Gerber of the 354th Fighter Group, based at Boxted near Colchester, was transferred to the Station's Sick Quarters.

That still left the 20 men from the two bombers unaccounted for and so another Walrus, piloted by Flight Lieutenant Sheppard and with Warrant Officer Errington as crew, took off to continue the search. Arriving at a position about 2 miles north–east of Walton they saw oil patches on the water. High Speed Launches and other small craft were busy in the area and the sea was quite calm. Flight Lieutenant Sheppard therefore returned to Martlesham.

On 11th March 1944 General Montgomery's tour of invasion forces in Britain brought him to Frinton and Walton. While waiting for his train, at the Southcliff end of Woodberry Way, the General looks out over Walton Pier. Scaffolding, erected against the invasion that did not come, still lines the beach between Winchester and Pavallion Breakwaters. *I. W. M. H36626*

Twenty men were not missing. The collision had been between two single seater 'Mustang' fighters. However, the confusion was not over yet, as just before midday another Walrus was despatched to search the area again, as the second Mustang involved in the collision was still considered to be missing. The situation was finally resolved when news came through later that the second Mustang had managed to make it safely back to base.

In a separate incident, shrapnel from anti–aircraft defence guns caused minor damage to the roofs of 15 houses spread throughout Frinton Kirby and Walton.

Thursday, 20 April

In the early evening, the naval authorities at Brightlingsea informed Walton Coastguards that some airmen were believed to be in a dinghy 3 miles off Walton. The lifeboat was launched and proceeded to the spot, accompanied by the motor boarding boat. No airmen were seen, but some soldiers were found fishing from a dinghy.

Wednesday, 26 April

A Mustang aircraft was reported to have crashed into the sea in flames about a mile off Holland Haven. The Clacton lifeboat was launched and what appeared to be a submerged aircraft was found, but there was no sign of the pilot.

Saturday, 20 May

The Dutch Minesweeper *M.M.S. 227* was mined and sank 10 miles east of the Naze.

Sunday, 28 May

An explosion at sea, of unknown origin, resulted in minor damage being reported to seven properties in Frinton and Walton.

Tuesday, 6 June

'D–Day', Allied Forces landed in Normandy.

Friday, 16 June

The first of many: a Flying Bomb (V1) was reported over the District heading towards Harwich. This was just three days after the start of the Flying Bomb campaign against London had begun. The pilotless aircraft were being launched from sites concentrated in the Pas–de–Calais region of north eastern France, and it can only be assumed that this particular machine was considerably off track.

Wednesday, 21 June

Just before 6 a.m., a Flying Bomb crashed in the sea.

Tuesday, 27 June

A Flying Bomb crashed in sea off Walton.

In the early evening, an American twin–engined P–38 'Lightening' fighter crashed just outside the District, at Landermere Quay, injuring the pilot.

Wednesday, 28 June

In the afternoon, three barrage balloons came down in the sea, two off Holland and one 3 miles east of Walton Pier.

Between June 28th and 29th, one Flying Bomb crashed in the sea in the vicinity of the Cork Light–vessel and another flew over the District in the direction of Harwich.

The record of Flying Bombs passing overhead or crashing in the sea is not complete and those mentioned hereafter should be looked upon only as examples of what took place. However, all those falling on land inside the District boundary or at sea close enough to cause damage, are mentioned.

Friday, 7 July

One Flying Bomb passed over.

Sunday, 9 July

In the evening a drifting barrage balloon was brought down at Holland Haven after it become caught in telephone wires.

Thursday, 13 July

One Flying Bomb passed over.

Tuesday, 18 July

One Flying Bomb passed over.

Wednesday, 19 July

One Flying Bomb passed over.

Thursday, 20 July

One Flying Bomb passed over.

Monday, 24 July

Two Flying Bombs passed over.

Tuesday, 25 July

Four Flying Bombs passed over.

Thursday, 28 July

One Flying Bomb passed over.

Monday, 31 July

One Flying Bomb passed over.

Tuesday, 8 August

A Spitfire crashed into the sea off Frinton. The R.A.F's. No.527 Squadron, operating out of R.A.F. Digby in Lincolnshire, was engaged in radar calibration duties. A variety of different aircraft types were used by the squadron for this task, including single engined Hurricanes and Spitfires and twin engined Blenheims and Oxfords.

On 8th August, Warrant Officer Arthur Herbert was flying a Spitfire MkVB, W3129, in formation with his Commanding Officer, Squadron Leader Potgieter. When just a couple of miles off Frinton, Squadron Leader Potgieter saw Warrant Officer Herbert's Spitfire turn and dive inverted into low cloud, apparently out of control. Nothing more was seen of the Spitfire. A search was conducted by other pilots from the Squadron and by the Air Sea Rescue Flight at Martlesham Heath, but no trace could be found of the missing aircraft or its pilot by the time bad weather forced the search to be called off. A further search the following day also revealed nothing and the 24 year old pilot was posted as 'missing believed killed'.

Some time earlier, Arthur Herbert had been recommended for promotion to commissioned rank. The recommendation had been approved and later, when his body was found, it was Pilot Officer Arthur Herbert who was buried in Cambridge City Cemetery.

Wednesday, 23 August

Explosions from unknown sources resulted in minor damage being reported to five houses in Frinton, Kirby and Great Holland.

Wednesday, 30 August

At a quarter past four in the afternoon, a Martinet target towing aircraft force landed at Manor Farm, Great Holland.

No.627 Squadron R.A.F. had by that time taken over Target Towing duties from 1627 Flight at R.A.F. Ipswich. During the afternoon of 30th August, Sergeant Hubert, a Polish pilot, was flying Martinet T.T.1, No.FM557, to Clacton. In the vicinity of Frinton and Great Holland the Martinet developed a problem with its engine. Sergeant Hubert was unable to increase the engine's speed and the aircraft began to loose height. Being at just a thousand feet there was not enough height to bale out and Sergeant Hubert brought the Martinet in for a forced landing in the open fields to the south of Great Holland. Once down, the aircraft caught fire. Sergeant Hubert and his crewman managed to get clear of the wreckage and escaped injury.

Home Guards carry out gun drill on a 3.7-inch Heavy AA gun at the Naze, April 1944. The men from Middlesex and Surrey were on a four day anti-aircraft gun course, which included shooting at an aircraft towed 'sleeve' target. Behind the gun is a line of rocket launchers. The photograph was taken on the top of the high cliffs to the north of the Naze Tower. In the autumn of 1944, during the Flying Bomb offensive, batteries of AA guns were established on the lower slopes of the Naze, further north. *I. W. M. H37486*

Tuesday, 19 September

Units from No.40 Anti–Aircraft Brigade began to arrive in the District.

In response to the increasing threat of V1, Flying Bombs, a 'gun belt' of anti–aircraft guns was being established along the Essex and Suffolk coasts. A distinction was also being made between zones where fighter aircraft could attempt to engage the Flying Bombs and where the guns would have a free hand. Many lessons had already been learned in attempting to combat the Flying Bomb threat after the previous few weeks experience further south on the Channel coast.

On 19th September, No.40 Anti–Aircraft Brigade moved from the south coast, at Eastbourne, and redeployed in the 'anti–diver' role along the coast between Clacton and the Naze – 'diver' being the military term then in use for the Flying Bombs. The Brigade comprised a mixture of Light and Heavy Anti–Aircraft units, the latter being equipped with 3.7-inch guns, deployed in batteries of eight guns.

The Brigade's Headquarters first moved to *Westwood House* in West Bergholt, but within a few weeks it had transferred closer to the coast, at *Hillcrest School* in Second Avenue, Frinton.

Initially three 'Heavy' batteries were deployed in the District: two at the Naze and one at Birch Hall, Kirby. There was one 'Medium' battery between Frinton and Great Holland and one 'Light' battery near Holland Haven. Two other 'Light' batteries were just outside the District, at Beaumont Hall and Landermere Hall, both having their Battery H.Qs. at Frinton.

At that time the 'anti–diver' batteries had restrictions on firing, being permitted to engage Flying Bombs only below 6,000 feet (3,000 to 4,000 feet being a usual flying altitude for the V1) and not, as a rule, to engage hostile aircraft. Fire was also restricted over the built–up area of Frinton and Walton, however that did not prevent the occasional rain of shrapnel from descending on the towns.

Wednesday, 20 September

Twenty six properties, scattered throughout the District, suffered minor damage as a result of shrapnel from the anti–aircraft guns: seventeen in Walton, six in Frinton, two in Kirby and one in Great Holland.

Saturday, 23 September

During the evening an aircraft was reported to be down in the sea in flames, some 8 to 10 miles south of the Walton Coastguard Station. At 9.53 p.m. the lifeboat was launched and together with the Clacton lifeboat, searched the area but found nothing.

By October the arrangement of the 'anti–diver' gun sites had been established as follows:

136 HAA Regt. (Regt. HQ – *Bentley Lodge,* The Esplanade, Frinton.)

409 Bty. at K6 Gunsite – *Birch Hall Farm* (Lane End side), Kirby–le–Soken
(Bty. HQ – *Coillesan,* Prince's Esplanade, Walton.)

182 Bty. at K7 Gunsite – The northern end of the Naze Golf Course.
(Bty. HQ – *Eastcliff Hotel,* Walton.)

432 Bty. at K8 Gunsite – The northern end of the Naze Golf Course.
(Bty. HQ – The Naze Golf Course Clubhouse.)

150(M)HAA Regt. (Regt. HQ – Jaywick.)

515 Bty. at C4 Gunsite – Between Gt. Holland Church and Frinton.

19 LAA Regt. (Regt. HQ – *St Annes*, Fourth Avenue, Frinton.)

294 Bty. at KA2 Gunsite – *Birch Hall Farm* (Skipper's Island side), Kirby.
(Bty. HQ – *Changi,* Fourth Avenue, Frinton.)

263 Bty. at KA3 Gunsite – Just west of *Creek Cottages*, The Naze.
(Bty. HQ – *Yellow Sands,* Cliff Parade, The Naze.)

Monday, 16 October

After so many Flying Bombs had passed overhead or had fallen short in the sea, the first damage in the District to be caused by one of them happened on this day. It was at about 8.10 p.m. when the explosion occurred, to the south–east of Lower Kirby. At first it was thought that it was a mid–air explosion, but whatever happened, the Flying Bomb separated into two parts.

What was probably the warhead came to earth some 500 yards south of the Walton–Kirby road and midway between Turpin's Farm and Turpin's Lane where it left a crater 20 feet by 10 feet. Ninety houses received minor damage, by far the majority being at the eastern end of Lower Kirby, with a few in Frinton Road (Kirby Cross), Halstead Road and in Walton. There were no casualties.

The following day the Flying Bomb's body and propulsion unit were found by the side of the road, 150 yards west of Ashes Corner. The remains, painted pale blue, were sufficiently intact for some writing to be decipherable, including the number 268069 which appeared on both the body and the propulsion unit, [probably the Flying Bomb's individual serial number].

Tuesday, 17 October

At about midday, a fighter aircraft was reported to be down in the sea off the N.E. Gunfleet. The lifeboat was launched to search the area, but nothing was found.

Just before 10 p.m., almost as a repeat of the previous evening, the explosion of a Flying Bomb destroyed by the anti–aircraft guns caused damage to property at the eastern end of Lower Kirby. Again the device appears to have separated. What was probably the warhead portion landed about 200 yards on the opposite side of the road to *Brick Barn Farm* at Lower Kirby.

Damage to property was more localised this time and mainly affected *Brick Barn* and *Devereux* farms and their associated cottages. *Brick Barn Cottages* in particular were badly damaged. There were no casualties.

The main body of the Flying Bomb, minus warhead and wings, was found half a mile to the north–east, in a field off the lower end of Rigdon's Lane. The propulsion unit and body were intact but damaged. Again markings were decipherable, this time the serial number on both parts was '251900'.

Wednesday, 18 October

For the third consecutive evening a Flying Bomb caused disruption in the local area. It was at 11.30 p.m. and this time the damage was more severe. The effect of the blast was centred on the seaward end of Pole Barn Lane, Frinton, where three houses were destroyed; *Little Croft* and *The Hay House* in Pole Barn Lane itself and *Sandy Hook* which fronted on to The Esplanade. Twenty three houses in the immediate vicinity were seriously damaged: in Pole Barn Lane, No.5 Council House, *Ostenda, Rudyard, Conway, Town End, Sea Glimpse, Sunny Cottage, Happy Days, Thorpe Villa, Pole Barn End, Roydon, Road End Cottage, South View, The Cliffs* and *Stay–a–While;* in Winchester Road, *Farnsworth, St Joseph's Convent, South Standing, Rayleigh Lodge, Winchester House, Ikthus* and *Mon Abri;* and in The Esplanade, *Hollywood.*

Elsewhere, in most of Frinton and Walton, there was widespread minor damage. In all, 545 properties were affected, either from the effect of the Flying Bomb's blast or from the associated anti–aircraft gunfire shrapnel. After such devastation it is perhaps surprising that there were only two slight casualties.

The Frinton Flying Bomb was one of three which came over that evening and fell within minutes of each other; the others came down just to the north–west of Weeley and just south–west of Aingers Green.

Friday, 20 October

At about 5.30 a.m., a Flying Bomb exploded immediately to the north of Stone Point at the Naze.

Saturday, 21 October

Just before 6.30 a.m., a Flying Bomb exploded in mid–air to the north–west of Lower Kirby, between Skipper's Island and the farms at *Birch Hall* and *Kentshill.* There were no casualties and no reports of damage.

Monday, 23 October

During anti–aircraft gunfire just before 8 p.m., a shell exploded at the Albion end of Walton High Street, causing minor damage to the *Albion Hotel* and three other properties in the vicinity. Elsewhere in Walton, shrapnel from the guns caused minor damage to ten other properties.

Wednesday, 25 October

A Flying Bomb fell in the vicinity of Walton at about 7.30 p.m., without causing any damage or casualties.

Monday, 6 November

The explosion from a Flying Bomb, just outside the District, caused minor damage to seven properties at Kirby.

Thursday, 9 November

Just after 7 p.m., a Flying Bomb fell into the sea off Walton after having been shot down by anti–aircraft gunfire. Three properties in Walton reported minor damage from shrapnel.

Friday 10 November 1944

A Flying Bomb fell into the sea off Walton at about 7.30 p.m. Sixteen properties between Walton and Frinton received minor damage from shrapnel and, in one case, damage from a defective anti–aircraft shell.

The partly fragmented nose-cone fuse from an anti-aircraft shell, found at the Naze. During air raids, 'taking cover' was not only from the effects of enemy bombs, but also from the rain of potentially lethal anti-aircraft shrapnel.

Monday, 13 November

Just after 6.00 p.m., a Flying Bomb fell into the sea off Walton without causing any damage or casualties.

Wednesday, 15 November

In the early morning, just after midnight, a Flying Bomb fell into the sea off Walton without causing any damage or casualties.

Friday, 17 November

An explosion at sea off Frinton and Walton was thought to have been from a V2, Long Range Rocket. Minor damage was reported to seven properties in Frinton.

Sunday 19, November

At about 8.30 p.m., a Flying Bomb exploded in mid–air over Walton after having being hit by anti–aircraft gunfire. There were no casualties and no damage was reported.

Friday, 24 November

Just before 6 a.m., a Flying Bomb exploded in a field just behind the junction of Halstead Road and The Street at Kirby Cross, causing widespread damage to properties in Kirby. There were no casualties and none of the damage was serious, but minor damage was extensive. The greatest concentration of damage was in the western parts of Kirby Cross and Lower Kirby.

In Kirby Cross, most properties along the Thorpe Road and in The Street were affected, including the Ministry of Food's food store at Royce's Garage; also a number of properties along the Frinton Road as far as Chestnut and Willow Avenues. Nearly every property in the length of Halstead Road recorded some damage, as well as most in The Street at Lower Kirby and some along the Walton Road at Lower Kirby, as far as and including Victoria Avenue and Quay Lane. In all, 289 properties recorded damage of some sort, together with another 14 in Frinton and Walton – these presumably the result of shrapnel from anti–aircraft gunfire.

Monday, 27 November

Explosions during the clearance of defence land mines from the cliffs at Walton, caused minor damage to ten houses at The Parade, Southcliff, South View Drive, Woodberry Way and Victoria Road. In most cases the damage was confined to broken windows.

Tuesday, 5 December

Shrapnel from anti–aircraft gunfire damaged the roofs of seven houses in Walton.

Sunday, 10 December

The anti–aircraft defences were again in action against Flying Bombs in the early evening. Just before 7 p.m. one Flying Bomb exploded over the sea a few hundred yards off the Albion beach at Walton. Thirty one properties in Walton received minor damage and a further nineteen had windows broken. There were no casualties.

Monday 11, December

Just before 11 a.m. an American Mustang fighter crashed into the garden of a house in Upper Third Avenue, Frinton.

The 503rd Fighter Squadron was one of the three P–51D 'Mustang' equipped Squadrons that formed the American 339th Fighter Group, based at Fowlmere near Duxford in Cambridgeshire.

Earlier that morning, the Squadron had taken off from Fowlmere on a mission escorting B–17 'Flying Fortress' bombers to Giessen in Germany. The Mustangs climbed out on a course directly for the rendezvous point with the bombers, near Liege in Belgium. Shortly after having made landfall near Ostend, Lieutenant John Gokey's Mustang developed an engine problem. He reversed course, dropped his long range fuel tanks and set course for Woodbridge, an airfield on the Suffolk coast used for emergency landings. As was usual in such situations, another pilot was detailed to escort Lieutenant Gokey home and in this case the duty fell to Lieutenant Bernie Allen, who takes up the story.

"After crossing into the continent near Ostend and prior to rendezvous with our bomber formation, Lieutenant Gokey radioed that his engine was running rough and that he would have to return to base. The formation leader, Captain Perry, instructed me to escort him back. We reversed course and started a slow let–down with Lieutenant Gokey leading. About half way across the North Sea he reported that his engine was getting rougher. The weather was pretty good with broken clouds and the sea had white caps. Visibility was about five miles.

As we came in sight of land he was having trouble maintaining altitude. About that time I saw a stream of black smoke coming from the lower part of his engine. As I moved under his plane to check the source of smoke, flames started to appear. I then told him that his plane was on fire and he should bale out. We were still over water, a couple of miles off shore.

He stayed with the plane until he reached land, then jettisoned the canopy. He banked a little to the left and bailed out, narrowly missing the tail section. I think the bail–out altitude was between one and two thousand feet. His 'chute opened and he landed safely near a house.

After seeing he was O.K., I flew on to Fowlmere and reported his location. When Lieutenant Gokey returned to Fowlmere, he said he landed in an English lady's garden. She greeted him with concern, hospitality and a cup of tea. Gokey also stated that he had no intention of jumping into a white capped sea on a cold day. All in all it was a satisfactory ending to what could have been a disaster."

Lieutenant John Gokey's 'English lady's garden' was in Pole Barn Lane. His Mustang, No.4415560 and coded D7–V, fell into the garden of *Raygarth* in Upper Third Avenue. The house was being used as a billet for troops at the time, but no one was hurt and remarkably the house only suffered superficial damage. Not surprisingly, the aircraft was a complete write–off.

The decision not to jump into the cold sea was probably a wise one, when one considers what happened just a month later off Clacton, during a similar situation of an aborting aircraft being escorted home. Then Flying Officer Raymond King of the American 436th Fighter Squadron, ditched his Mustang just offshore by Clacton Pier. The Clacton lifeboat was launched straight away and just a mile east of the Pier picked up the already unconscious pilot. He was given artificial respiration and although still alive when brought ashore, he died later in hospital.

Tuesday, 12 December

Windows in four houses on The Esplanade at Frinton were broken during the clearance of defence land mines.

11th December 1944, the remains of John Gokey's P-51D Mustang, 44-15560, coded D7-V, lie in a Frinton garden, before removal by USAAF authorities

Photos. via John Harris

Lieutenant John Gokey

Lieutenant Bernie Allen

1945

Wednesday, 3 January

During the demolition of defence landmines on the seafront at Frinton, the public shelter on the greensward opposite Oxford Road was severely damaged.

Shrapnel from anti–aircraft gunfire caused minor damage to four houses in Kirby and Walton.

Saturday, 6 January

In the morning, during the outbound leg of a bombing mission to Germany, a four engined B–24 'Liberator' from the American 448th Bomb Group developed a mechanical fault. The crew baled out safely, leaving the aircraft to its own fate. The pilot, Lieutenant Sampson, landed at Simpson Farm Dovercourt. Just after 11 a.m. both the Royal Observer Corps and the A.R.P. recorded a Liberator aircraft as having crashed into the sea between the Naze and Landguard Point.

Tuesday, 9 January

During the demolition of defence land mines at Frinton, minor damage was caused to the golf clubhouse and *West Point* at the southern end of The Esplanade.

Wednesday, 10 January

During the course of the day two American aircraft made forced landings at Great Holland.

At 10.45 in the morning, a P–47 'Thunderbolt' force landed between Hodgnoll's Farm and the railway line just to the north. The pilot was safe. In all probability the aircraft came from the 62nd Fighter Squadron which was part of the 56th Fighter Group based at Boxted, just to the north of Colchester.

David McLaren's history of the 56th Fighter Group, "*Beware The Thunderbolt*", based on the official U.S. records of the unit, relates the events of that morning when the Group was despatched on a 'fighter sweep' over the continent, as part of the protecting force for an American bombing mission. Soon after take–off from Boxted, the formation leader had to turn back and not long afterwards, "..Flight Officer Walter Sharbo, of the 62nd Fighter Squadron had to make a belly landing at Clacton. He was uninjured.." In all, 17 of the Group's 54 fighters despatched had to return early from this particular mission.

By early afternoon the formations of bombers were homeward bound, some marked by the effects of enemy fighters or anti–aircraft gunfire. Struggling to make the coast was a B–17 'Flying Fortress' of the 860th Bomb Squadron, part of the 493rd Bomb Group temporarily based at Little Walden, near Saffron Walden in north–west

Essex. The pilot brought the massive four engined bomber down in the fields to the south of Great Holland, the aircraft finally coming to rest with its nose close to the main Clacton road across the marshes.

The damage to the B–17 was considered repairable on site and so preparations were put in hand to make the aircraft airworthy and to fly it out. The alternative would have been to take the whole machine apart and transport it by road. The visitor became a familiar site during the next couple of weeks while the work progressed and it did not take long for word to spread amongst the local schoolboy community, many of whom had gained a passion for things aeronautical, having been fed a constant visual diet of streams of aircraft heading out over the coast almost daily.

Albert Scott was then a thirteen year old living at Burrs Road, Clacton. The B–17 was just a cycle ride away and he was to make a number of visits before the repair teams got to work. Although the aircraft was guarded by the Americans, a blind eye would be turned to the inquisitive youngsters as they came and went through the rear hatch. He well remembers the thrill of going inside for the first time and sitting in the pilot's seat. Evidence of what brought the bomber to Great Holland lay in the fragmented remains of the 'plexiglass' nose cone and the blood stained bomb aimer's position; at least one engine was also damaged.

While the aircraft was being repaired, men from the U.S. 861st Aviation Engineering Battalion, based at Boreham near Chelmsford, worked on the nearby fields preparing the temporary runway. After a few weeks, when all was ready the mighty aircraft took off, heading in the direction of the Frinton coast, for a somewhat overdue return to its unit at Little Walden.

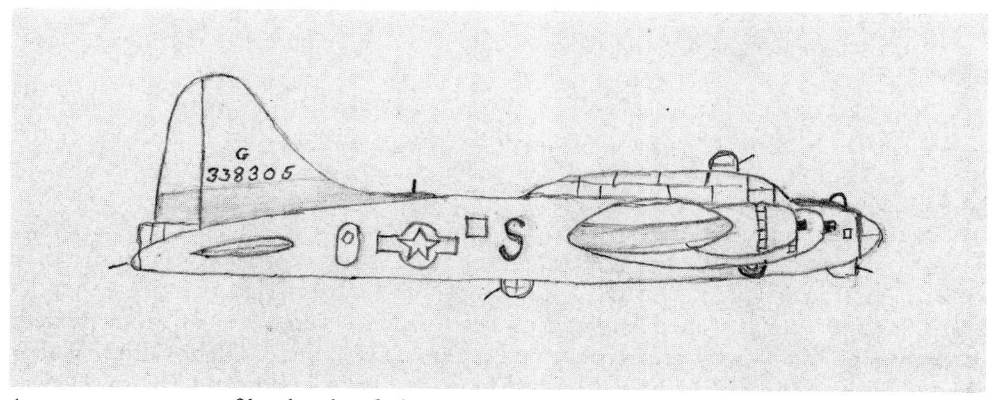

A contemporary profile sketch of the Gt. Holland B-17 made by a young local R.A.F. Serviceman Norman Nugent. The shaded bands are red unit markings. *Norman Nugent*

Friday, 12 January

Shrapnel from anti–aircraft gunfire caused minor damage to five properties in Frinton, Walton and Kirby Cross.

Saturday, 13 January

A Flying Bomb fell in the fields half a mile to the south of Great Holland Church just after 6 a.m. There were no casualties and no damage to buildings.

Wednesday, 17 January

In the early evening the lifeboat was launched to search for a parachute reported down in the sea between Frinton and Clacton. However the lifeboat was recalled when information was passed by the naval authorities at Brightlingsea that an aircraft had dropped a container by parachute and that it was not an airman.

Saturday, 20 January

The Walton Coastguards received a report from the Navy that a 'Flying Fortress' had come down in the sea just offshore to the north of Clacton. The lifeboat was launched to search the area, but returned having seen nothing. The R.N.L.I. later reported that the aircraft had come down just inshore on flooded marshland.

Whether this was a case of duplicate reporting of the B–17 which had force landed ten days earlier at Great Holland and was being repaired there, or another B–17, is not known. Besides the basic requirements of salvage and making good damage, the removal of crashed aircraft prevented multiple reporting of incidents which could tie up valuable resources and waste time and effort.

Sunday, 28 January

A V2, Long Range Rocket, exploded at 7.30 a.m. in the vicinity of the Wade mudflats, to the north–east of Lower Kirby. Damage to buildings was slight and consisted mainly of broken windows to some 19 properties in Kirby and Walton.

Whereas the V1 Flying Bomb could almost be classed as a pilotless aircraft, the V2 Long Range Rocket was a true ballistic missile.

The V1 was either ground launched from ramps or air launched from underneath specially converted bombers. It flew relatively low and straight until its engine cut out, then it fell to earth. It could be destroyed by fighter aircraft or by anti–aircraft fire.

The V2 was fundamentally different and there was no effective defence against it. It fell out of the sky from high altitude on the downward leg of its ballistic trajectory, begun with a vertical launch from a site on the other side of the southern North Sea.

Saturday, 10 February

At 9.47 a.m., an explosion at sea damaged the windows of five properties in Frinton and Walton. The source of the explosion was thought to have been from the destruction of a V2, Long Range Rocket.

Monday, 12 February

The explosion of a V2, Long Range Rocket, over the sea caused minor damage to three properties in the District.

Saturday, 17 February

At ten minutes to one in the morning, a V2, Long Range Rocket, fell just outside the Frinton & Walton District boundary at Kirby, between the Thorpe Road, Pork Lane and the railway line. Some cottages were demolished on the Thorpe side of the boundary and in the Frinton & Walton District, 37 properties were slightly damaged, most being along the Thorpe Road at Kirby Cross. There were four slight casualties in the Frinton and Walton District.

Sunday, 18 February

Just after 6 p.m. a V2, Long Range Rocket, fell in part of the defensive minefield at the Naze. There was no damage to property and there were no casualties.

Thursday, 22 February

A V2, Long Range Rocket, fell outside the District in the Clacton area. The local A.R.P. Rescue Party was sent to assist with first aid repairs. Shrapnel from anti–aircraft gunfire caused minor damage to nine properties in Walton and Frinton.

Saturday, 3 March

Just before 5 a.m. a Flying Bomb exploded in the air over Walton Road, between Central Avenue and the Frinton railway gates. Minor damage was caused to ten properties in the nearby Frinton Park Estate, six of which were in Grace's Walk. A number of small explosive incendiary bombs were found in the vicinity and were assumed to have come from the Flying Bomb as none of them were found to have tail fins fitted. Elsewhere, but primarily in Walton, there were a further 30 cases of minor damage, probably the result of anti-aircraft shrapnel. There were no casualties.

Tuesday, 6 March

Shrapnel from anti–aircraft guns caused minor damage to four houses, two in Lower Kirby and two in Walton.

In the early hours of the morning an allied bomber crashed at the Naze, on the reclaimed marshland to the north–west of Creek Cottages.

The previous afternoon, just after 16.30, eleven 'Halifax' bombers from 432 (Leaside) Squadron R.C.A.F. had taken off from Eastmoor in Yorkshire, as part of a large Bomber Command force bound for Chemnitz, deep inside Germany.

The operation did not get off to a good start. A number of aircraft joining the force from other airfields nearby, crashed soon after take–off and the resulting loss of life was considerable. The poor weather conditions were to blame; a combination of low cloud and bad icing conditions.

The weather continued to prove as much a hazard as the enemy's defences. During the return flight, strong winds were encountered and as the journey progressed, fuel states must have become a concern for some aircraft. Only two of 432 Squadron's aircraft made it all the way back to Eastmoor that night, landing at 02.35 and 02.48, after flights lasting a gruelling ten hours. Eight others put down at airfields in the south and east of England, but one of the squadron's aircraft was missing.

Later, Halifax RG475 was found to have crashed at Walton at 01.20 hours, after having been engaged by our own anti–aircraft guns. Whether hit by the gunfire or forced into a catastrophic manoeuvre to avoid it is not recorded, but the result was the same and the four engined bomber fell to earth at the Naze, killing all on board. How could such a tragedy have occurred?

Since the introduction of the 'anti–diver' (Flying Bomb) defences – a continuous strip of anti–aircraft guns along the coast from London to Norfolk – there had always been the possibility of conflict between the requirements of the defending guns and the safe passage of allied aircraft. Various measures had been put in hand to overcome the potential dangers. By the beginning of March 1945 an instruction was in force forbidding all flying by friendly aircraft below 8,000 feet over the 'gun strip', both by day and by night, except under certain conditions when the restrictions could be lifted. The low flying zone was thus left clear for the instant reaction required of the gunners against Flying Bombs and possible night intruders.

Additionally, it became common practice to route allied bomber formations around the gun zone, away from the southern North Sea coast. A route via southern England and northern France, although increasing the flight time to a target, kept the aircraft clear of the east coast defence zone and also had the advantage of reducing flying time over hostile territory as the allies advanced further eastward in mainland Europe.

Two nights previously, the Luftwaffe had mounted a large scale night intruder operation which had met with considerable success, targeting Bomber Command's airfields and bombers returning from their night sorties. That event, coupled with the continuing vigilance against Flying Bombs, probably resulted in a heightened state of alert along the 'gun strip'.

On the night of 5th/6th March, as was now quite normal, the bomber stream had flown south from Yorkshire, passing west of London and out over the south coast before turning east towards the target area. The return flight was planned to follow a similar track, making landfall at Beachy Head.

It is speculation, but the only really logical explanation for a lone aircraft being over the northern Thames Estuary, so far from the main bomber stream route, is if it had been damaged in some way, had fallen out of formation and, alone, became unable to fix its position properly. Flying low, not through choice, and probably unable to give the correct recognition signals, the wounded bomber ran into the heightened alert state of the anti–aircraft 'gun strip' and thus the tragedy unfolded. Seven Canadians and one Briton died when Halifax MkVII RG475, coded QO–L, crashed at the Naze. Besides the normal crew of seven, an additional pilot was being carried to gain experience.

It was not an isolated incident, as the previous day a Liberator had been shot down by anti–aircraft gunfire off Frinton and in March a Flying Fortress engaged by the guns had crashed at Wrabness.

The crew that night, and the number of operational trips made by each man, were as follows:

Pilot	S/Ldr Edwin A. Hayes, R.C.A.F.	16
Pilot (Addit.)	F/Lt John G. Clothier, R.C.A.F.	1
Navigator	F/O Colin M. Hay, DSO, R.C.A.F. (age 31)	19
Air Bomber	P/O Joseph D. Ringrose, R.C.A.F. (age 23)	14
Wireless Op.	F/Lt Glenn R. Harris, R.C.A.F. (age 25)	8
MU. Air Gunner	F/Sgt Marius B. Nielson, R.C.A.F. (age 19)	14
R. Air Gunner	F/Sgt Gilbert M. Orser, R.C.A.F. (age 19)	11
Flight Engineer	Sgt Douglas M. Cooke R.A.F. (age 21)	14

Flight Lieutenant Clothier was buried at Pentwyn in Wales, the remaining seven are together at the Commonwealth War Graves Cemetery at Brookwood in Surrey.

Above: S/Ldr. Hayes and his original crew, probably an 'arrival on squadron' photograph. Later, F/O Hay *(below left)* took over as navigator from F/O Hemming. F/O Hay had been awarded the DSO, the citation for which is recorded below.

One night in September, 1944, Flying Officer Hay was the navigator of an aircraft detailed to attack Bottrop. It was his third operational mission. Whilst over the target, the pilot was severely wounded and lost control of the aircraft which went into a dive. Displaying great promptitude, Flying Officer Hay took over the controls and succeeded in levelling out although inexperienced as a pilot and despite the fact that some of the instruments were unserviceable. He flew the aircraft back to an airfield and landed it. On touching down the undercarriage collapsed and the aircraft caught fire, but the crew got clear uninjured. This officer displayed great coolness and resource and was undoubtedly responsible for the ultimate safety of his comrades.

A salvage party may have removed larger sections of the Halifax wreckage, but otherwise the remaining debris and heavier items, such as engines, propellers and undercarriage were buried at the crash site in shallow pits. Over the years, parts of the wreckage became exposed on the surface of the reclaimed marshland *(see below)* and in 1973 members of 308 Squadron (Colchester & Clacton) Air Training Corps organised an excavation at the site and recovered many of the larger items. Three of the aircraft's propeller blades were subsequently made into a memorial, erected in 1978 in the Memorial Gardens opposite Walton Parish Church by the Frinton & Walton Branch of The Royal Air Forces Association *(see opposite)*.

The remains of Halifax RG475 in 1966. *Above*, fragments litter the marsh surface, including an undercarriage leg in the foreground. *Below*, three of the four Bristol Hercules radial engines.

Left, 50 years on. Wreaths from the 50th anniversary commemorative service lie at the R.A.F.A. memorial by Walton Parish Church.

Friday, 9 March

Just after midday an American Mustang fighter crashed at the eastern end of Thorpe Park Farm, between Pork Lane and the railway line. The pilot baled out and was injured. The aircraft was completely destroyed.

Monday, 12 March

A V2, Long Range Rocket, crashed at 11.15 a.m. just outside the Frinton & Walton District boundary, to the west of Lower Kirby, between Lane End and Dale Hill. Two casualties were taken to hospital where one later died. Two houses outside the District boundary were destroyed. Damage to property inside the District was limited to the western end of Lower Kirby, where there were eight instances of minor damage.

Thursday, 15 March

During the day the explosion of two Flying Bombs and shrapnel from the anti–aircraft guns, resulted in minor damage to three houses in Walton. Three more had windows broken.

Wednesday, 21 March

During anti–aircraft gunfire against Flying Bombs, minor damage affected 41 properties in the District, mainly in Frinton and Walton.

Thursday, 22 March

At about 7 a.m., a Flying Bomb, hit by anti–aircraft gunfire, fell a quarter of a mile north–east of Great Holland Hall, between Frinton and Great Holland. There were no casualties and no damage resulted. Numerous small burnt–out incendiary bombs were found in the vicinity.

Monday, 26 March

Just before 4 a.m. a Flying Bomb, hit by anti–aircraft gunfire, glided out of the District towards the west.

Thursday, 29 March

Anti–aircraft gunfire was intense and at just two minutes into the new day the barrage was rewarded with a Flying Bomb being brought down in fields three quarters of a mile west of Hodgnoll's Farm at Great Holland. The Flying Bomb was packed with small incendiary bombs, but caused no damage to property or casualties. However, the intensity of the anti–aircraft gunfire resulted in minor damage to 84 houses throughout the District, mainly in the Walton area. As with other such incidents, the price was small when compared with the damage that might have been caused had the Flying Bomb completed its mission.

This was the final incident to affect the Frinton and Walton Urban District and the remaining five weeks of the European war were free of incidents.

The Reckoning

Over 47 properties were destroyed or had to be demolished as a result of bombing and a similar number were seriously damaged; hundreds sustained minor damage, many on more than one occasion.

Casualties were 12 killed, 17 seriously injured and 51 slightly injured.

Walter Lowther–Kemp's A.R.P. Incident log recorded 1094 occasions of air raid alerts and 179 A.R.P. 'incidents'. A monthly list of ordnance that fell in the District was also kept, the final summary being as follows:

348	High–explosive bombs
-	Incendiary bombs (numerous) *
12	Parachute mines
12	'Oil' bombs
12	'Firepots'
11	V1, Flying Bombs
3	V2, Long Range Rockets

* Entries stopped at the end of 1943 when the total was 297 [probably because of the difficulty accounting for such small objects which could be delivered in such a variety of forms – individually, grouped in a canister or combined with other explosive devices].

Frinton & Walton A.R.P. Rescue & Repair Party, primarily men connected with the building trade.

Left to right

Back row:

Bill Candler, Eric Luff, Stanley Pinner, ______ McHale, ______ Relf.

Middle row:

______ Chapman, Cliff Downes, ______ ______, Jo Marshall, ______ Brown, Frank Candler, ______ Smith–Gillard.

Front row:

Vic Blake, ______ Eastaugh, ______ ______, ______ ______, Bill Rich.

Home Guardsmen: Kirby Platoon, 'D' Company, photographed on Gt. Bentley Green.
Susan Whipp

Left to right

Back row:

Ernest Coote, John Stooke–Vaughan, Harry Elvish, Fred William, Tom Slowgrove, Sid Whipp, ______ Hempson, Ray Pinner, Fred Hudson(?), ______ ______, ______ ______.

Middle row:

Cory Harris, Frank Glading, Eddy Harris, Charles Martin, George Cockrell(?), ______ Harris(?), Abe Potter, Hubert Maddison, Arthur Bugg(?).

Front row:

Sam Scott, George Townes, Walter Miller, Bert Flemming, Jack Wilson, Stan Martin, Bill Theadom, Herbert Kay, Frank Grey.

Walton Air Training Corps *Gordon Blease*

Left to right
Back row:

Gordon Blease, ______ Cordwell, ______ Nunn, Ken Strange, John Nicholls, Bobby Bocking, George Hawkes, Louis Culpin.

Front row:

Charles Hawkes, Ian Bartle, Peter Smith, H.C. Benson (C.O.), Roy Keeble, ______ Caesar–Gordon, Ken Haydon.

Walton Auxiliary Fire Service, outside their depot in Mill Lane.
Rosemary Oxborrow

left to right
Back row:
George Wood, C.T. Christmas, Bill Coombs, ______ ______.

Front row:

______ ______, Jack Hicks, ______ ______.

NOTES